ARTHUR ROBERTS

A TEACHER'S JOURNEY

ELIZABETH BUTEL

Research by Elizabeth & Geoff Hunter
and Sandra Roberts

ETT IMPRINT
Exile Bay

I have the honor to be
Sir
Your obedient servant,
A R Roberts.
Teacher.

This edition published by ETT Imprint, Exile Bay 2016

ETT IMPRINT
PO Box R1906
Royal Exchange NSW 1225
Australia

Copyright © Elizabeth Butel, 2016

ISBN 978-1-925416-36-7 (ebook)
ISBN 978-1-925416-37-4 (paper)

Design by Hanna Gotlieb

CONTENTS

PREFACE

Arthur Robert Roberts was a schoolmaster and it was education and the changing nature of the educational system that shaped his life. Born in the hop-growing region of Kent, his life and prospects were transformed by a wave of educational reform that carried him far from family, class and country. To that extent, he was a creation of England's early attempts at a national school system, set up to prepare workers for the growing and diversifying industrial system and the explosion of printed matter that came with it.

If he had remained in England, this transitional role may have been manageable. In choosing emigration, he was condemned to an unstable teaching life, often in one-teacher schools in crude outposts. There, he came under the watchful eye of local patrons and subject to the directives of embattled administrators, trying to make the most of government funds. Far from the surety of family background, he found himself on the frontier of attempts to establish a national school system in Australia. With a swiftly growing family – one child with a severe disability – he was transplanted from one struggling district to another, fighting insolvency, ignorance, natural disaster and bitter sectarian divides. These last were to leave deep marks within the family, with both Arthur and his son Arthur William (also a schoolmaster) confirmed agnostics.

His letters to the Board, later Council of Education, requesting school-room furniture, upgrades to buildings and teaching assistants give some insight into his frustrations. Records in the Council's archives charting his progress and decline give others. Photographs and family folklore reveal a taciturn, deeply flawed man while the evidence of his writings (as Scone correspondent for *The Maitland Mercury*) suggests a fiery intelligence and defiant pride. This is amplified by a portrait of Roberts in Havelock Ellis's autobiographical novel, *Kanga Creek*.[1] There, the schoolmaster, Mr Williams, is portrayed as an educated and passionate agnostic who uses the pen name *Anti-Humbug* when writing letters to *The Stockwhip*, a journal possibly modeled on publications like *The Bulletin*.

This narrative presents these contradictions and hopefully gives the reader some sense of Roberts' life.

---

[1]   Kanga Creek, Havelock Ellis, The Golden Cockerel Press, England 1922

Origins

David Roberts and Sarah Philpott - married Maidstone Kent
7/10/1832 - Children

David, born East Farleigh Kent 24.04.1833

Frederick, born East Farleigh Kent 17.07.1835

Katherine, born West Farleigh

Kent 23.12.1837 Arthur, born East

Farleigh Kent 29.05.1840

Henry, born East Farleigh Kent 26.03.1843

John, born East Farleigh Kent 20.07.1845

Sarah, born East Farleigh Kent 8.08.1847

Samuel, born East Farleigh Kent 7.09.1851

Born in 1840, Arthur Roberts was the fourth of a family of eight children, living at 10 Lower Street in the village of East Farleigh, Kent.[2] David Roberts, Arthur's father, was born in nearby Barming while his mother, Sarah Philpott, was born in West Farleigh. The district, referred to in that era as 'the Garden of England' had been associated with intensive cultivation of hops for over 200 years.

In English census records of the period and notations on marriage and birth certificates in Australia, David Roberts is described as an agricultural labourer, or gardener and hop farmer, contributing to Kent's supply of hops to British breweries. This was by no means a peaceful rural occupation for the dried flowers that gave beer its characteristic bitter odour and flavour were a vulnerable crop, plagued by pests and fluctuating prices. In Arthur's childhood, the plants grew on wooden frames, replaced in later years by strings of wire. It's likely he joined in the hop picking, for the

[2]   Ref Batch Number CO36591, Dates 1580-1840, Source Call Number 0845114, Film 6906441

Ref Grant Thompson gt@austarmetro.com.au

Ref Sandra Roberts sandraroberts@bigpond.com

season often engaged the whole family, meaning he shared in the heavy manual work and the convivial celebrations that marked its end.

Harvest time in August drew scores of itinerant workers to the district for a strenuous working holiday. These seasonal workers (some from the slums of London's East End) were organized into teams and paid according to a tally system, based on the number of baskets picked. This tally became a site of conflict for the more militant out-of-towners, with strikes and protests erupting intermittently throughout Arthur's youth. Thus, he had the dual influence of witnessing his settled environment disrupted by industrial strife and the social abuses and eccentricities brought by a motley collection of gypsies and town dwellers.

Further disruption was caused by a disastrous cholera outbreak in Kent in 1849. Starting in Arthur's own village, it killed 33,000 people across the wider districts and felled 43 itinerant workers in East Farleigh in one blow. These unfortunates were buried in a mass grave in the village cemetery, an occurrence that must have made a grim impression on the local population. Cholera was endemic in an era of unregulated water supply and local villagers were likely grateful for the plentiful supply of beer. The latter was regarded as a healthy alternative, nutritious and 'harmless' and drunk by adult and child alike (although children's drinks were early examples of 'light' beer – brewed to have a low alcohol content).

Moreover, the Beer Act of 1830 had been introduced with the specific intention of reducing the public drunkenness created by gin palaces and substituting premises which sold only beer. Even proponents of the temperance movement saw beer as a normal accompaniment to a meal. By Arthur's birth year there were nearly 50,000 beer houses.[3] Indeed throughout his life in England such taverns were the norm and good profits could be made by those who conducted them.

---

3   http://www.britainexpress.com/History/oast-houses.htm

In an essay in *The New Statesman and Nation*[4] no less a writer than George Orwell has left a lengthy description of hop picking, recording the spiny stems of the plant that cut the palms of the hand and the plant-lice that crawled down the picker's neck. Nonetheless, he believed there was *"on hot days … no pleasanter place than the shady lanes of hops, with their bitter scent—an unutterably refreshing scent, like a wind blowing from oceans of cool beer."* However, as Orwell noted, this romantic vision was punctured by the meager living derived from hop picking, owing to bad seasons and employers' abuse of the tally system.

In theory, a good picker could earn a reasonable living but nature and man generally conspired to make sure he didn't. Bad weather, unfair measurement and hops that varied in size from hazelnuts to small pears all contributed. Whole families could work ten hour days for little reward and what amounted to starvation wages. Workers could be sacked at the whim of the farmer and 'docked' for work already done if they walked off the job. At the end of a day's work, the Roberts' family at least had their own home but for itinerant workers the accommodation was primitive, often a mere stables with little protection from wind and rain.

Orwell has also left a detailed description of hop picking in one of his lesser-known novels, *A Clergyman's Daughter*[5]. Disoriented by amnesia, the heroine finds herself on the road and linking up with a trio of East Enders, making their way down to Kent for the season. There she sleeps rough in huts filled with straw, where sundry female hop-pickers bed down for the night. Her days are spent picking hops, in ten and twelve hour stints. They breakfast at 5:30am on fried bread, bacon and tea then form partners or teams for the day's work - pulling hops off the bines, detaching stalks and leaf matter and trying to avoid the tiny thorns that tear their hands. The early part of the day is slow work as the hops lose their dew, followed by a productive period in the late morning when they are easier to handle. An

---

4   New Statesman and Nation, 17 October 1933

5   A Clergyman's Daughter, George Orwell, Victor Gollancz 1935

hour's respite for lunch is followed by more picking until 5-6pm, with the mindlessness of the work tempered by singing and camaraderie. At the end of the day, stupefied with tiredness, the workers' hands are covered in *"coal-black filth"*, which can only be removed by mud or the hop juice itself.[6]

It is a vivid and daunting picture but it is reasonable to assume that home pickers, such as the Roberts' family, would have been among the more efficient and thus best paid workers, their income supplemented by agricultural labour outside the hop picking season. David Roberts, Arthur's father, may likely have been one of those regular laborers who tended the plants as they grew, becoming adept at stilt-walking to manage the growth at the top of the bines. These traditions are evident in the occupation of several of Arthur's siblings. David, the eldest, was a sawyer and ship's carpenter; Frederick, the second son, was a gardener and agricultural labourer; Henry, the fourth son, was also a sawyer and comments made in Arthur's Scone writings suggest his own detailed knowledge of trees and plants.

---

6   Ibid, Orwell, Chapter 2, pp108-121

Early Schooling

According to East Farleigh's History Society, the first school in the village was held on the church porch – effectively a Sunday school where local children were taught to read. [7] From 1820-1846, a National School was established next to the Old Vicarage. This was an offshoot of *The National Society for the Education of the Poor* and not part of the state sponsored national system of later decades. The state had yet to assume responsibility for education and such early schools were set up by the Anglican Church and funded by public subscription and charity trusts.

We can only speculate about the education the Roberts' children may have received in these institutions but the dates suggest that the greater part of Arthur's schooling would have taken place at a new school set up by the Reverend Henry Wilberforce in 1846.

How was it that he came to be lifted out of the family's world of manual labour into the realms of the professions? The answer lies in the social changes that were transforming England during this period.

England in 1850

For the more enlightened politicians, social reformers and industrialists of the mid 19th century, education was one answer to the growing social distress and economic upheaval of Britain's transition from an agricultural to an industrial economy. Widespread and irrevocable change was underway, with the abolition of slavery, economic and parliamentary reform and the 'People's Charter' calling for universal male suffrage. [8] As patterns of village and family life were disrupted and often permanently fractured, education was seen as one way to prepare new generations for the marketplace and the society developing around it. Theoretically, education

---

[7]   East Farleighs' History Society, Duncan Spencer Chairman, East Farleigh Network 2009

[8]   Coincidentally, two ministers at the Roberts' family parish church were sons of William Wilberforce, the pivotal spirit behind the abolition of slavery.

was the pathway to averting crime, poverty and social disorder and it was supported by reformers from different backgrounds and social classes.

The growth of large towns also called for a new form of local government which could deliver efficient systems of public sanitation, public health and public education. The concentration of poorly educated men and women seeking work had led to various abuses and it was little wonder that reformers saw the need to educate them so they could comprehend the changes taking place. The growth of the textile mills had led to the abuse of child labour but had also promoted the reforms of the Factory Acts of the 1830s, with education as something of a by-product. Children aged 11-13 years were to work 9 hours/day and a 48 hour week, with attendance at some form of schooling for 2 hours/day. Those aged 13-18 years were restricted to 12 hours work/day and a 69 hour week.[9]

What schooling options were available for these young people? Wealthy citizens favoured private tuition with governess or tutor, whereby their children would not be 'tainted' by contact with the lower echelons of society. Some middle class families used fee-paying grammar schools but for working class families, with few financial resources, there were limited choices. The fee-paying private academies were of dubious worth and Parish and Charity Schools were only available in some areas. The Education Act of 1833 had provided funding to build state sponsored schools but even if these eventuated, many areas lacked the administrative apparatus to enforce children's attendance. The result was that many children did not attend school at all. Furthermore, country children did not necessarily share the reforms of the Ten-Hours Bill, passed in 1847, which restricted the working hours of women and children. It was clear that state sponsored national schools could address these many inequities but how would they function in a climate of religious controversy over what form of scriptures should be taught?

_____

[9]   England in the 19th Century, David Thomson, Pelican History of England No 8, p47

The decades before and after Arthur's birth, were marked by the fight for religious equality and an end to preferential treatment for Anglicans over Protestant Dissenters and Roman Catholics. Along with educational inequities, these groups had been largely excluded from ministerial or administrative office, from admission to the universities and from commissions in the armed services.

How did these volcanic social upheavals affect life at the village level in East Farleigh, Kent and in particular, the education of Arthur Robert Roberts? The family was Anglican, attended regularly and sang in the choir so Arthur and his siblings were well suited to the National School, sited (till 1846) next to the Old Vicarage of St Mary's Church. That year new premises were built next to the church itself, the result of a subscription-drive by the Reverend Henry Wilberforce.

This was doubtless in response to a dramatic population increase in the village (c.1500 in 1830) due to increases in hop production.[10]. It was most probably here that Arthur received his first elementary schooling and here where he showed the promise of above-average ability, leading to his appointment as a pupil teacher in 1853.[11]

December 1846, when Arthur was six years old, marked a further watershed in British education for this was the year a comprehensive system of state-supported apprenticeship and teacher training was set up.[12] Under this system, inspectors could nominate able students of at least 13 years of age to undertake a five year apprenticeship under approved school masters. Such students became salaried pupil teachers, assisting the school

---

[10]   Duncan Spencer, Chairman, East Farleighs' History Society, East Farleigh Network

[11]   Cited in Department of Education Records, Archives Authority of New South Wales AO Reel 1991 Education Department Teachers' Roll 1869 1908 Vol 1 record number 886

[12]   The politics of working class education 1830-1850 by Denis G Paz, Manchester University Press, 1980

master with daily classes and receiving tuition for at least one hour at the end of the school day. In exchange, the pupil teacher was paid £10 for the first year of training, while their instructing master was eligible for an annual stipend. If the pupil teacher continued successfully, their salary rose in annual increments of £2.10s. Further scholarships (created by government gift) were available for intensive training at a Normal School in the final years of study, with such candidates attending institutions like the Training School set up at Battersea in 1840.

This pupil teacher arrangement was modeled on successful systems in Holland, Edinburgh and Glasgow where the pupil teachers acted as teaching assistants, receiving instruction from the schoolmaster then carrying this instruction to the wider group. It allowed large groups of children of diverse age, ability and needs to be catered for, often in one long schoolroom. But it was an unsatisfactory system in so far as the pupil teachers were often not much older than the students they taught. In an era of widely used corporal punishment, if the pupil teachers were female and/or physically smaller, there might be further abuses, leading to anxiety and intimidation. Pupil teachers who made it through to the training schools were clearly successful in mastering these difficulties.

Training schools were often referred to as Normal Schools in this period since they established the 'norms' of teaching standards. Successful trainee teachers studied at them for up to 3 years and served as pupil teachers at village schools linked to the institution. This was a much longer period of trained apprenticeship than comparable pupil teachers in newly established colonial Normal Schools for many years. If applicants were successful in their final examinations they were indentured for 2 years and became salaried assistant teachers in selected Pauper Schools.

In spite of these innovations, there remained competing educational claims from sectarian interests, with the Anglican Church by now fighting to maintain its position within sectarian education. The National Society that had been set up to represent Anglican interests was joined by the British Society, set up to maintain the interests of other sects. These two societies promoted their own curricula and teachers and each utilized their own textbooks. The state-sponsored national system proposed secular classes followed by an hour of religious training from different denominations at the end of the school day. Periodically, inspectors would visit schools to monitor the progress of secular training but they would have no control over religious teaching. The first government grants of 1833 had funded the building of schools and the payment of salaries but new reforms provided for textbooks, school furniture, school masters' accommodation, playgrounds and gardens.

An obituary for Arthur Roberts published in 1898 stated he had been educated at Chelsea College, London, where he was fortunate to receive *"personal instruction in mathematics from the noted Dr Colenso and in music from Hullah"*.[13] It is difficult to verify this claim as research has so far failed to reveal records for Roberts at the Training College named. Furthermore, Dr Colenso was living in South Africa for most of the relevant period. A partial explanation may be that Hullah and Colenso were both noted educators of the era, with methods of instruction that became the model for some of the Normal Schools. Colenso had been a tutor in mathematics at the Harrow School and later taught at St John's College, Cambridge. He published a series of books on mathematics, with his book on arithmetic in wide use. Therefore it is possible that Roberts was referring to college training in the methods of Colenso and the inference that this was *"personal instruction"* mistakenly came from his family. A simpler explanation is that he inflated his training to help secure a better position in the colonial system, a common practice for many who emigrated to make a new life.

Arthur's claim that he received instruction from the composer and teacher John Pyke Hullah (a specialist in vocal music and composition) is more credible. Hullah had been commissioned by the educational reformer, Sir James Kay-Shuttleworth, to give classes on Wilhem's method

---

[13]   Maitland Daily Mercury, 22 February 1898

of instruction at the newly opened Normal School for Schoolmasters at Battersea and later gave classes at Exeter Hall for schoolmasters and the general public, as well as classes at some of the great public schools. Classes also took place at St Martin's Hall Long Acre where Hullah later lived. He was lecturing publicly throughout the 1850s and 1860s, making Roberts's claim to personal tuition within the realms of possibility. Hullah's later role as Musical Inspector of Training Schools for the United Kingdom gives further credence as do the many references to Arthur's teaching of vocal music while schoolmaster at Scone and Maitland. His obituary notes he was *"very fond of music and was a good performer on different instruments"*. He is also reputed to have been an organist in England and to have initiated a band at Inverell.

If Arthur's progress followed the standard form, he would have completed his five years of training in 1857-58. An indenture period would follow, wherein he practiced his skills at a selected school and gave back to the state some of the benefits of his training. His letter of April 1861, addressed from Falcons' Rest on Auckland's North Shore, corroborates this, noting he had served his five year apprenticeship in England, followed by service as a master of a National School for nearly two years.[14]

This letter also reveals the reason behind Arthur's emigration. *"... my health giving way I was advised abroad,"* he writes; a statement later supported by Havelock Ellis's recollections in *Kanga Creek*, a novel dealing with Ellis's time as a teacher in country New South Wales. We have no knowledge of the nature of this health breakdown but we do know that together with his elder brother David, Arthur set sail for New Zealand in June 1859. Once again, according to his obituary (which wrongly places his arrival in New Zealand in 1857) Arthur had passed a competitive examination required by the New Zealand Government and soon he was teaching on Auckland's North Shore.

---

14   State Records, Education Department, Western Sydney Records Centre, Kingswood NSW, Reference Number and Title 2/9280 8761

The family history archives of Auckland City Libraries list David and Arthur Roberts as passengers on the *Matoaka,* a wooden, full-rigged ship of over 1000 tons.[15] The vessel had departed from Gravesend England on 15 June 1859 and arrived in Auckland, via Wellington late that September. As Elizabeth Hunter points out in her comprehensive and detailed time-line of Arthur Roberts and his wife, Elizabeth Houston, various immigration schemes were in place in New Zealand during these years. Some of these provided assisted passage aimed at increasing the ranks of skills and professions in the fledgling society. Schoolmasters would, doubtless, have been in high demand as would sawyers and ship's carpenters, the trades professed by Arthur's brother David.

We are fortunate regarding records for Arthur's brief time in New Zealand. His name is mentioned as witness to the Will of William Trevarthen (dated 8 December 1859). Trevarthen, a settler on the North Shore of Auckland, had been wounded by a horse the day before and felt compelled to make his will. Three witnesses are listed: Arthur Robert Roberts, Schoolmaster, North Shore; Thomas Duder, Signal Man, North Shore and George Burnett, Shipsmith, North Shore. Trevarthen made his mark as signature but, as a literate and educated man, Arthur signed the will in the manner characteristic of his existing correspondence. The jury lists for Auckland for 1860-61 also list an Arthur Roberts, schoolmaster, resident at Albert Street Auckland.[16] Arthur was only 19 years old when he emigrated. His brother David was 26. Thus, it seems not unreasonable to speculate that part of his passage from England included employment on arrival in Auckland, where he appears to have remained for well over a year. His letter from Falcons' Rest mentions he had held his present school for the previous 18 months. For his part, David may have been attracted to New Zealand by the discovery of gold in 1859, with further discov-

15   The Southern Cross, 27 September 1859, Ref Grant Thompson gt@austmetro.com.au

16   The Southern Cross, 7 February 1860

eries in 1861. His skills as ship's carpenter and sawyer would be usefully employed both on the journey out and on the fields and settlement that accompanied them.

Once again, thanks to efforts by members of the Roberts' family such as Grant Thompson and Sandra Roberts, a further mention of an *A. Roberts* has been found in the passenger lists of *the Otago Witness*, published out of Dunedin Otago in the relevant period.[17] The vessel was the steamship, *the Lord Ashley* and Roberts was travelling in a second class cabin. If this *is* Arthur Robert Roberts then it would place him in Otago in April 1861. The lists for October 1859, when we believe Arthur was teaching on the North Shore of Auckland, had also listed a Roberts, who may or may not have been David, Arthur's eldest brother. Certainly if David had settled temporarily in Otago, it seems natural that his younger brother would join him there prior to leaving New Zealand. *The Nelson Examiner and New Zealand Chronicle* (15 June 1861) reports the presence of A. Roberts in a second class cabin of *the Lord Ashley*, which had departed Nelson for Sydney on 12 June. Other documents (State Records Authority NSW) list Roberts among the arrivals in Sydney, disembarking from *the Lord Ashley* on 20 June 1861.

The Maori wars were causing civil unrest throughout these years and coupled with personal choices of which we have scant knowledge, this may have influenced Arthur to continue his journey of discovery to New South Wales. A further temptation is to speculate on the appearance of the names Gavin Houston (farmer of North Head, Auckland) and Gavin

---

[17]   Ref Grant Thompson gt@austarmetro.com.au, Ref Sandra Roberts sandraroberts@bigpond.com

Houston Jnr, in the jury lists for this period.[18] If Arthur had become acquainted with the relevant Houston family during these years, his early marriage to Elizabeth Houston in December 1861 would seem more comprehensible. The couple was married within six months of Arthur's arrival in Sydney, with the bride's father Gavin Houston and brother, Gavin Houston Jnr as witnesses. It would further explain why Arthur left New Zealand for Australia in the middle of 1861, if his intention was to pursue a relationship already in progress.

Certainly, in a letter from Falcons' Rest he cites the following as reasons for his application and intention to settle in New South Wales: *"My friends all have left here and settled in Sydney..."*[19] He queries the qualifications needed to obtain a school in Sydney and whether his certificates from England will be sufficient, noting that he had gained a further certificate of proficiency in New Zealand. On the evidence of a letter dated 18 February 1862, he must have forwarded these and other testimonials the previous August.[20] The letter requests their return, while a further notation at top left records the return of a Certificate of Merit on 24 February 1862. No record of these has been passed down to the family and we can perhaps assume that, along with many other valuable documents and possessions, they were lost in the Maitland flood of 1893.

The name of Arthur Robert Roberts as Temporary Assistant Teacher at the William Street National School late in 1861 testifies to the success of his application, as does a report from the Examiners to the Secretary of

---

18   Elizabeth Hunter traces the Houston family history In her timeline for Arthur Robert Roberts and Elizabeth Roberts, noting that Gavin Roberts may have tried farming in the Hinton area in the early 1850s. If so, the speculation that he may be the Gavin Roberts, Farmer, of North Shore Auckland becomes marginally stronger.

19   The letter was written in response to an advertisement in the Sydney Morning Herald calling for schoolmasters for National Schools.

20   Letter to C.W. Wills, Secretary Board of National Education, Sydney, requesting the return of testimonials and certificates.

the Board of National Education, dated 13 September 1861. The Report carries the signatures of the two examiners, Mr T. Harris and Mr William Wilkins, at that time Chief Inspector and destined to become one of the most influential figures in the development of public education in New South Wales. [21]

"… Mr Roberts has been regular and punctual in his attendance, correct in manner and appearance, docile and attentive to instruction and diligent in study. He has been very useful in supplying the places of Teachers who were absent on account of sickness or engaged in examinations.

…Mr Roberts natural ability seems to be above the average, and to have been fairly cultivated by instruction in the ordinary school subjects and by some amount of reading. He has further received a considerable amount of training for the profession in which he has long been engaged. We estimate his attainments as follows:

Grammar	-	Tolerable
Geography	-	Fair
Arithmetic	-	Good
Art of teaching	-	Tolerable
Lesson Books	-	Fair
Reading	-	Moderate
Writing	-	Fair
Euclid/Music	-	Examiner's Report not yet received

…As a teacher Mr Roberts evinces more intimate acquaintance with the details of the profession than a majority of candidates and manages a class with fair skill. He exhibits promise of becoming a teacher of more than average efficiency.

---

[21] Reel 4108, No 70 Education Department School Files Archive, State Records, Western Sydney Records Centre, Kingswood, NSW

...Reviewing the whole of Mr Roberts' qualifications, we are of opinion that he should rank in Class 11, Section B as a National School Teacher, We propose to leave the question of his appointment till a future opportunity."

Soon after, on 27 September 1861, Arthur Roberts was appointed Temporary 3rd Assistant Schoolmaster at William Street National School.[22] He later requested a formal copy of his certificate, which listed him as Class 2A.[23] Within ten weeks, he was married, lending further credence to the notion that he was already in some form of relationship with Elizabeth Houston.

The same document that lists Arthur's temporary appointment at William Street National School also lists several other names. Regarding a Mr W.H. Miller, of Bendameer, the following is noted: *"This candidate is not yet married and I would not personally recommend his appointment unless he could be accompanied by a wife. W. McIntyre, however, is of the opinion that W. Miller would succeed as a single man. It would perhaps be well to consult the Local Patrons on this point."*

Married men were preferred due to the isolated nature of many postings. A wife would support the schoolmaster in his teaching endeavours and would likely provide sewing and other instruction to female and younger children. She would be homemaker and companion and an insurance against the schoolmaster forming an inappropriate attachment to a pupil.

Arthur Robert Roberts, aged 21, married Elizabeth Houston, aged 19, at St Barnabas Church in Parramatta Street Sydney on 4 December 1861.[24] Within months they were making the journey south so Arthur

---

[22]   Reference Number Item and Title 2/92808761, State Records, Western Sydney Records Centre, Kingswood, NSW

[23]   No copy of the certificate has been located and it may also have been lost in the Maitland flood of 1892.

[24]   Now known as Broadway, Sydney

could take up the post of Schoolmaster at the Croobyar National School, near the town of Milton. It is possible that the suddenness of this distant posting led to the need for a special licence by which the couple could be married without the usual delay of three weeks for the announcing of the bans. [25]

Croobyar 1862

Soon after Roberts' arrival in Australia he was a married man and within months, a father.[26] These personal revolutions were mirrored by larger revolutions within the education system in New South Wales. With great deliberation and with great difficulty, schools were being set up in newly emerging centres of population and Arthur's progress, as he moved from one rural district to the next, followed the unsteady course of the new national system.

As a schoolmaster sent by the Board of National Education to these outposts, his job was not just to educate the scholars but to maintain and develop the newly established school against the competing claims of family farms and the implacable opposition of rival church schools. If he could not maintain an enrolment of above 30 pupils, in all probability, the school would close. His personal circumstances (married teachers were preferred) and his character would be significant. By his leadership and example he would convey the superiority of the public system over the poorly trained and potentially divisive nature of its denominational competitor.

He would work alongside local patrons whose role it was to oversee school buildings, pupils' fees and manage parental enquiries and/or complaints. These patrons would work in partnership with the schoolmaster,

---

[25]   Marriage Registration Transcription, Reference Number 1861/831, Church Register 303

[26]   David Arthur Gavin Roberts was born on 16 July 1862; Ulladulla birth registration number 14175

acting to support him in requests to the Board of Education and to keep a diligent eye, both on him and his charges.

As early as 1849, the character of the ideal teacher had been described as *"a person of Christian sentiment, of calm temper and discretion … imbued with a spirit of peace, of obedience to the law and loyalty to the sovereign and not only (possessed) of the art of communicating knowledge but … capable of moulding the mind of youth"*[27]

The national system was being developed along British lines. In 1848, responsibility for the building and maintenance of schools and for schoolmasters' salaries had passed from the Clergy and School Lands Corporation, to the Board of National Education and the Denominational School Board. The former was responsible for establishing the public school system, for teacher training and classification, and for setting up model schools. The latter would manage distribution of government subsidies to new and existing church schools of different denominations.

The Model School would be attached to a training college and plans for this were set in motion, with the conversion of the old military hospital at Fort Street in Sydney's Rocks District, with William Wilkins as its first headmaster. His job, allied to that of the inspectors who were put in place over the following decades, was to transform the shambling status of education in New South Wales into a coherent, unified system which would eliminate the inequalities then in place. Schools were *"squalid and inefficient beyond belief. Most of the teachers had no professional training; were uncouth, illiterate and brutish. They used excessive corporal punishment and were a disgraceful example of personal conduct."*[28]

Wilkins' conviction was based on his own tours of inspection, where he had found himself *"appalled at the plight of the Australian child"*.[29] He acquired a powerful ally in these years in Henry Parkes, whose humble

---

[27]   Australian Education 1788-1900, A.G. Austin, Pitman 1964, p48

[28]   Ibid, Austin, p57

[29]   Ibid Austin, p55

origins and Chartist sympathies had convinced him of the need to support public education. However, the cost to government would be high, with a school building at that time likely to cost at least £150-200 to plan and build. Furniture, materials and equipment would be needed and of these heavy sums, the community – and especially its most prosperous citizens - would be expected to pay one-third. Fees might be set at £6/year for boarders and £2/year for day pupils.

Croobyar School was opened in June 1862, some fourteen years after these momentous changes. The school was sited on David Warden's property, close to Croobyar Creek. *"In those days Croobyar Road led from East Milton (where Hackett's restaurant stands today) in a straight line to the creek".*[30] Warden operated the Croobyar Estate, the largest in the district and had established a National School at Ulladulla in 1861.[31] Now, along with other patrons such as William Ewin and Thomas Hobbs, he wanted to provide a building for children of tenants in the Milton area.

Along with Boolong and Broughton Creek, Croobyar was considered to have a good schoolhouse *"erected at the sole cost of the owners of the estates upon which they are situated."*[32] This private ownership meant it was classified as a non-vested school, with different terms and conditions. The state provided furniture and materials and paid the teacher's salary. Originally textbooks were those used in the Irish National System and British and Foreign Society but the need for local content led reformers like William Wilkins to write their own geographical and other texts. The schoolbooks from the Irish system were considered far superior to those used in Anglican schools, created by the Society for the Propagation of the Faith, and the Catholic Series, created by the Christian Brothers and used in Catho-

---

[30]   Tales Out of School, p31

[31]   The Croobyar Estate was 2,560 acres

[32]   Extract from Report of the Council of Education Upon the Condition of Public Schools, Kiama Family History Centre

lic schools.[33] The Irish texts had been written to instill literary and moral knowledge, *"Christian in content but free of dogma. There would be no Bible but there would be scripture extracts."* [34]

When the young Arthur Roberts and his bride arrived at this first posting on the south coast of New South Wales in 1862, the school had an enrolment of 30 boys and 23 girls and most of them attended regularly. When they were safely housed in the new location and the inspector visited that July, almost all the girls were present and 24 of the boys. The inspector reported that Croobyar was well supplied with all the necessary materials and that the moral character of the school was excellent. Instruction was carried out judiciously and the teacher's methods were *"fairly skilled."*

"Fair proficiency has been attained for the time the school has been in operation", he wrote.[35]

In our age of superlatives where even the most commonplace event is deemed 'awesome' we might wonder at the somewhat faint praise offered in these assessments. In fact, the ranking system which evolved during these years to describe the progress of a school or its master was measured to a fault. It consisted of three levels – good or fair, tolerable or moderate, indifferent or bad. To be deemed *"fairly skilled"* or of *"fair proficiency"* was to be placed among the higher levels of the growing system. Many schools and their teachers were frankly awful - ill-equipped with resources, housed in inferior buildings, administered by schoolmasters with rudimentary training.

According to these reports, school began at 9am, with two thirds of pupils *"reasonably punctual"*. In the main, these pupils were farmers' chil-

---

[33] Ibid Austin, p55

[34] Ibid Austin, p45

[35] Ibid, Kiama Family History Centre

[16] Ibid, Kiama Family History Centre

dren and various (sometimes onerous) tasks had to be performed before they left for school. In times of family illness or stress, pupils might be absent altogether. *"…..In more than half of the schools the regularity may be considered fair,"* the district inspector reported, *"but in many others the poverty of the people and the usefulness of the older children on the farm are strong inducements to the parent to detain them at home"*

This meant that almost half the students who attended school were less than 7 years old and a further proportion, less than 8 years. Once again we will leave it to the district inspector to describe the reasons behind this.

"In tending cattle, working in the corn field or supplying the place of hired labour, many weeks and even months are spent. The unfortunate pupils have scarcely returned to school when they are again called away … forget the little acquired during their brief stay, and lose all interest in knowledge for the time. Indeed in some schools the teacher's work is ever beginning and until some strong remedial measures can be devised, I see little prospect of alteration."[36]

Such difficulties made the teacher's role critical and much was expected of them. By comparison with many country teachers Arthur Roberts was well qualified, having received the full complement of training. He came into the New South Wales system as a Class IIA teacher which compared favourably with many teachers sent to country districts. The Board of National Education was struggling to establish a well qualified teaching force in these years and many of those operating one teacher schools in out lying areas were lacking in the higher skills of music and mathematics. It was a fact often cited in their failure to achieve promotion to a higher teaching grade.[37]

Inspectors' reports for 1863 deal only briefly with Croobyar, noting that the roll call comprised 24 boys and 18 girls, a slight reduction on 1862. The average attendance was even lower, numbering 23 boys and 13

---

[36] State Records, Western Sydney Records Centre, Kingswood NSW

[37] Archives Authority of New South Wales AO Reel 1991 Education Department Teachers' Roll 1869 1908 Vol 1 record number 886

girls. Other notes for the Central District deal generally with schools in the area so we have no way of knowing which of these notations referred to Croobyar. The inspector noted that two-thirds of school sites were well chosen, centrally located, well placed for pupils and *"healthy"*. In view of David Warden's special attention to the Croobyar site, we can assume it was one of these. Other schools in the district were deemed *"in most respects unsuitable"*. Playgrounds attached to newly opened schools were good but some attached to non-vested schools were *"too small to be of any real benefit. Others are insecurely fenced and unprovided with out offices of a suitable kind."*[38]

Lack of earth closets was considered an inducement to laxity and immodesty. *".....The cultivation of decency ... is greatly hindered by the manner in which most of these (out-buildings) have been placed. The entrances of many are so exposed that boys and girls cannot avoid seeing each other enter and leave them. In such cases, I have suggested alterations to effect proper separation and complete concealment."*

Non vested schools were sometimes *"scantily"* or unsuitably furnished, with a meager supply of equipment and books. Apparatus, books and records could be *"meager rather than unsuitable but teachers of careful habits are seldom without a good stock of books and the more useful maps at least"*. Given that attendance was the keystone for survival and growth of the school, attendance records were vital and the Board believed some teachers were deficient or deliberately lax in this regard. *"... comparatively few teachers attach sufficient importance to this matter"* they wrote. [39] Although his record was to be marred by various transgressions, Arthur Roberts was never accused of this laxity, a significant achievement in over thirty years of continuous service.

---

[38]   Extract from Report of the Council of Education Upon the Condition of Public Schools, Kiama Family History Centre

[39]   Ibid, Kiama Family History Centre

The government and tone of local schools varied widely with schools located in a town likely to be larger and more disorderly than their country counterparts. Four out of five teachers were *"fairly competent as regards attainments and attentive to their duties. With few exceptions they receive suggestions willingly and carry them out to the best of their abilities. Of the others some have not been fully and fairly tried and there are those of whom I cannot speak in terms of satisfaction."*[40]

Such broad brush descriptions are useful for grasping the unstable nature of the education system in this era. Much depended on the schoolmaster and his training but equally, the character of the local community was a significant factor, and their willingness to help develop the school and support children's attendance and behaviour. The religious affiliations of the community were also significant, especially in the decades ahead as churches became even more militant about retaining independent church schools.

In encouraging the spread of national schools, the Board of Education insisted on the involvement of the local community as overseers, as well as a substantial financial contribution of one third the cost of buildings and materials. The Board would pay the teacher's salary, expecting this would be supplemented by two-thirds of school fees paid. The roving inspector would correct accidental or deliberate abuses and further instruct schoolmasters on what was expected of them as regards educational standards for New South Wales.

The young Roberts family was increasing in these years with a daughter, Maggie, born at Ulladulla in 1864 and a second son, Arthur William Henry, born in March 1866.[41] Birth certificates for the children reveal that in these years, for reasons unknown, Arthur Robert Roberts advanced his age by two years. From this time on, including in his obituary and death

---

[40]   Ibid, Kiama Family History Centre

[41]   Maggie; Ulladulla birth certificate registration numbers 15492 and 15562 respectively

certificate, he is cited as two years older than his actual age. Elizabeth's remained unchanged but overnight she became four years younger than her husband rather than two.[42]

The companionship of Arthur's brother John may have eased his isolation in these years. John Roberts had emigrated to Australia at some time during these years and his name appears in the Ulladulla Directory for 1867. He was some five years younger than Arthur and soon to marry Sarah Whatman at Wandaree, Ulladulla in 1868.

Changes were also taking place at the administrative level of the education system, with the Board of Education becoming the Council of Education in 1866. The new Council controlled expenditure and government grants, establishing and maintaining public schools, and appointing, training and examining teachers. It set up local Boards to replace the old role of patrons, with these new entities responsible for visiting, reporting and inspecting on their school. At the same time a new classification - the provisional and half-time school - was created to deal with areas where pupil numbers were insufficient. School sites, buildings and furniture for these would be provided by the parents of enrolled pupils.

These provisional and half-time schools occupied a lower echelon than a full-time school and were referred to in some Council records as 4th and 5th class schools. Teachers were threatened with demotion to these if they failed to satisfy the Council on a number of fronts: failure to present themselves for examination for a higher teaching classification; poor governance in the running of the school; excessive use of corporal punishment and sundry moral failings. Removing a schoolmaster to a distant and less established school appears to have been both a form of punishment for wrongdoing and a practical solution to the problems caused by lack of trained teachers in remote or inhospitable districts.[43]

---

[42]   She was born 27.06.1842

[43]   Archives Authority of New South Wales AO Reel 1991 Education Department Teachers' Roll 1869 1908 Vol 1 record number 886

Arthur wrote to the newly formed Council in October 1866, informing them of an outbreak of *"a contagious distemper"* in the Croobyar district.[44] This was identified as *varioloid*, a mild form of smallpox occurring in people previously or infected with the disease. The local doctor had ordered him to close the school for a fortnight. Dairying districts were beset by disease in this era, with tuberculosis, for example, believed to be contracted in some cases in milk and dairy products from infected cattle. The primary infection could occur in childhood and while the bacillus was contained, the subject remained infected. The dormant condition could reappear in adulthood, either through re-infection or triggered by another disease. Childbirth was particularly dangerous since it activated the disease to enter a chronic secondary phase. For this reason many affected people were encouraged not to marry lest they develop 'galloping consumption' and seal their fate.

Maggie Roberts, still at this stage a young child, was to die of phthisis (another name for tuberculosis) in December 1893, at the early age of 29. The supposition that her condition was chronic is supported by her death certificate which lists the duration of the illness as one year. Her single status is a further pointer, for in spite of considerable beauty and a sociable nature, she did not work outside the home and died unmarried.

Family folklore points to a fiery relation between father and daughter in the years preceding her death. Marjorie Roberts (younger daughter of Arthur William Roberts) believed Maggie's lively social life and attendance at local dances and entertainments caused conflict with her father. She related a story, apparently told by her own parents, that Maggie's condition had worsened after her father locked her out of the house one night for returning too late from a dance. In view of the circumstances, it is a credible story, but like all family folklore, cannot be substantiated. However, this is to jump too far ahead in the story and for the present

---

44   Reference Number Item and Title 2/0280 8761, State Records, Western Sydney Records Centre, Kingswood NSW

we must return to the nuts and bolts of Arthur's struggle to maintain an enrolment above 30 at the Croobyar School.

After some decline in 1863-64, there was a jump in enrolments around the time of his departure. The inspector's report of August 1868 noted that *"the teacher's residence is too small. A class-room is needed and the whole premises should be repaired and cleaned. The discipline is good. All the prescribed subjects are taught. The teacher is intelligent, energetic and painstaking. The proficiency is fairly satisfactory."*[45] But this teacher was Arthur's replacement. With his family and pregnant wife, he had left the district late in 1867.

---

[45]   Extract from Report of the Council of Education Upon the Condition of Public Schools, Kiama Family History Centre

Insolvency

There is no reason to suppose that his removal to Glen William (in those days a journey of nearly 300 miles) was forced. Arthur may have applied for a transfer because the present posting was too small for his growing family's needs. A memo in Department of Education Archives notes he was appointed to his new posting at Glen William on 19 July 1867, but the family did not travel north until November-December of that year.[46] No doubt he tried to prepare for the move, but the fact remains that he was unable to settle a series of outstanding debts before departure. In addition, he accumulated debts along the way. The result was that on 18 December he filed as an insolvent, a move that would protect him against debtors threatening summonses. Under the rules of insolvency, his assets would be handled by an official assignee.

Arthur's Creditors and Claimants were owed substantial amounts – a series of 14 debts, adding up to £85.7.3. The deficiency, when £12.0.0 was subtracted for the value of property, was £68.11.0. It was not an auspicious start for the family in the new posting.

A series of letters to the Supreme Court of New South Wales and related documents record the details. The journey north to Glen William took place over the school holiday period and Arthur filed for insolvency from Clarence Town, a few miles south of his new school.[47]

"I am the above named Insolvent," he stated, *"and I am a Teacher residing in Clarence Town in the Colony of New South Wales –*

The cause of my Insolvency and the reason for my filing my schedule is in consequence of a Verdict obtained against me in the District Court holden at Nowra and execution having been threatened to issue for the sum of £10.7.11 being the balance of Verdict and costs in an

---

46   Reference Number Item and Title 2/9280 8761, State Records, Western Sydney Records Centre, Kingswood NSW

47   Insolvency Records File 2/9280 8761 State Records, Western Sydney Records Centre, Kingswood NSW

action brought against me by William Sturrocks residing at Ulladulla and being also threatened to be sued by others of my creditors and I am therefore compelled to sequestrate my estate for the protection of the whole of my creditors –"

The documents make uncomfortable reading for later generations as they give insight into the struggle of this young family to survive. The value of their furniture (exclusive of bed and bedding) was appraised at £3.18.0. In all, liabilities were £85.7.3; assets £16.16.3. A letter of January 1868 noted he had been asked to attend a meeting of creditors in Nowra the following month but that this was wholly impracticable. *"I have the honor to inform you that it is utterly impossible for me to attend, the distance being nearly 300 miles and I have no money to travel with."*

He commented on his insolvency in the letter, saying it was caused by *"undue pressure of my creditors. I owed Sturrocks £11.1.5. I have sent him £6.5 and still the debt is by court expenses £10.7.11. Marks also threatened to summons me and I therefore with my lawyer's advice sought the benefit of this Act."*[48]

Bailliere's Post Office Directory, 1867 gives the following details about his creditors.[49] Mr Sturrocks was a Postmaster at Ulladulla; Mr Marks was a storekeeper. In all, the Roberts' family owed debts to ten Ulladulla locals; four were storekeepers, one was a butcher, one a postmaster, two were innkeepers and two were farmers. These details and the debts owed give some insight into the family's needs.

Mr Hall, storekeeper	£15.7.4
Mr Sturrocks, Postmaster	£10.7.11
Mr Hession, farmer	£8.12.4
Mr Marks, storekeeper	£6.3.6
Mrs Tydeman, innkeeper	£6.3.6

---

[48]   Ibid, Insolvency Records File

[49]   Balliere's Post Office Directory, 1867, Internet History Resource, ihr.com.au

Mr Maloney, butcher	£5.12.4
Mr Martin, storekeeper	£5.3.4
Mrs Kennedy, storekeeper	£3.10.8
Mr J. Hession, innkeeper	£3.3.6
Mr Ewin, farmer	£2.10.8

In light of later developments, the substantial debts owed to two inn-keepers, Mrs Tydeman and Mr Hession (amounting to nearly £10) suggest the young schoolmaster had already developed a habit of drink. The family had additional debts to four Clarence Town locals. One of these, Mr Thomas Higgs, was a surgeon.[50] Of the others, one was a storekeeper, one a bootmaker and one the poundkeeper.

Mr Thomas Higgs, surgeon	£2.15.6
Mr W. Johnston, storekeeper	£13.15.6
Mr G. Johnston, poundkeeper	£2.10.6
Mr V. Bridekirk, bootmaker	£1.10.6

The Shoalhaven creditors duly met in February 1868 where the official assignee informed them that the value of the insolvent's furniture was £7 and apparel £5. *The above are the only assets in the Estate except a few worthless book debts –"*

A list of debtors was held with the documents. Some debts were listed as *"good"*; some were *"bad or doubtful"*. The amounts range from £1-2, down to smaller amounts of 5-15 shillings. We can assume some of these were probably parents, indebted to the schoolmaster for unpaid fees. The total of debts was £4.16.3.

Glen William 1867

According to *Glen William Public School, 1849-1974; Historical Account* by J. Burns-Woods, the school was set up in 1849 to cater for children of local tenant farmers growing wheat and other crops. It was some twenty years old when Arthur was first posted there. Since this was less than two

---

[50]   Elizabeth Roberts was pregnant with her fourth child Albert and, in view of Albert's disability, it is possible the surgeon's fees were in connection with her pregnancy.

years after widespread changes brought about by the Council of Education, it may be useful to consider some of these here.

The new Council was anxious to develop the pupil teacher system, whereby students received daily instruction from the schoolmaster as part payment for their services. This would allow bigger enrolments and ensure the supply of future teachers for an expanding national system. They stipulated that instructing schoolmasters must hold a second class certificate to ensure training was of the required standard. As with the English system, pupil teachers would begin at 13 years of age but would continue for the next four years, as opposed to a five year apprenticeship. Their *"aptitude and general fitness for the office of teacher"* would be tested over a three month probation period and they would sit for yearly examinations.[51] From 1867, if they had completed four years of successful study, the Council would admit them to a training school.

The head of the Council, William Wilkins, was particularly anxious for teachers to work to a Table of Minimum Attainments by which their students' progress could be reliably measured. To achieve this, teachers must be trained to deliver lessons based on sound principles. The Public Schools Act of 1866 had designated two training schools for this purpose. Teachers applied for admission to a training school via quarterly entrance examinations and if successful, attended 1-6 months. In practice the usual period was three months but this was amended in the 1870s to a training period of 6 months.

---

[51]   Council of Education Archive, State Records, Globe Street, Sydney

Course of Instruction at the Training School

Reading	with dictation and derivation
School Book	knowledge of the School Series of the Irish National Board to end of Third Book
Grammar	Parsing and analysis, and the elements of composition
Geography	Physical and descriptive
School Management	Organization, discipline and method
Arithmetic	Simple and compound rules, vulgar and decimal fractions, reduction, practice, and proportion
Drawing	Free-hand and elementary perspective
Music	Tonic-sol-fa method, the requirements for elementary certificate

These details date from 1871 when further refinements to the training system were in place, Candidates attended the Model School one day/week to receive practical training. Male candidates received instruction in military drill and female candidates in callisthenic exercises.[52]

The Council also stressed the importance of regular inspections of vested and non-vested schools alike. In this way they hoped to standardize instruction and ensure the worst abuses of excessive corporal punishment and indifferent teaching could be eliminated. Inspectors were in charge of separate districts and responsible for all schools affiliated with the national system in that area. In optimum conditions, the round of inspection would mean each school was visited at least once a year. In practice the time period was sometimes longer as it was common for inspectors to be responsible for 50-100 schools. Inspections might take place over two to three days and added to travelling times, it was a prohibitive schedule.

---

52   Extract from Report of Council of Education Upon the Condition of Public Schools, Kiama Family History Centre

Districts	No of schools or depts.	Number visited	Number unvisited
Albury	46	41	5
Armidale	87	67	20
Bathurst	89	76	13
Braidwood	92	89	3
Camden	104	88	16
Cumberland	85	80	5
Goulburn	96	81	15
Maitland	81	68	13
Mudgee	50	44	6
Newcastle	94	83	11
Sydney	108	108	...
Total	932	825	107

School inspection table for 1871-72[53]

At these inspections students were assessed in reading, writing, arithmetic, grammar, object lessons and geography. The schoolmaster was assessed in subjects taught, school management, the maintenance of school books and the teaching of linear drawing and vocal music. Post 1868, assessments in the Art of Teaching and English Literature were also included.

The following table gives insight into what was assessed in 1871-72 and the standard of proficiency reached. Writing and arithmetic skills appear to be in advance of reading in every category. The low figures for grammar and geography at elementary and advanced levels reflect a much smaller body of students tested and presumably taught. The subjects grouped in the final category are also revealing. Object lessons, drawing, music and needlework appear to have been widely taught but Euclid, algebra, mensuration and Latin have much lower numbers. One imagines that such 'higher' subjects might only be taught in some of the larger city and town

53   Ibid, Kiama Family History Centre

schools, with country schoolmasters struggling to teach basic skills in the three Rs – reading, writing and arithmetic.

Subjects taught and number of children examined in them					
Subjects	Estimated Proficiency				
	Good	Fair	Tolerable	Moderate to Indifferent	Totals
Reading					
Alphabet	867	970	1,191	1,763	4,291
Monosyllables	2,484	4,154	3,366	2,080	12,034
Easy Narrative	2,408	4,186	3,464	1,870	11,878
Ordinary Prose	2,878	4,586	1,715	796	9,925
Writing					
On slate	8,976	5,482	4,268	3,060	16,781
On copybook	6,100	7,658	4,125	1,524	19,407
Arithmetic					
Simple Rules	8,262	4,517	5,646	9,158	22,587
Compound do	1,015	1,311	1,808	2,801	6,435
Higher do	585	764	874	571	2,794
Grammar					
Elementary	1,484	3,084	2,729	4,014	11,311
Advanced	1,753	2,479	2,246	1,752	8,280
Geography					
Elementary	1,567	3,318	4,177	5,146	14,208
Advanced	1,634	2,655	2,205	2,068	8,562

Other subjects					
Scripture	1,962	2,759	1,646	1,196	7,563
or Moral Lessons	4,384	9,741	10,377	11,109	35,611
Object Lessons	2,031	6,793	5,354	3,547	17,725
Drawing	3,769	7,158	5,514	9,707	26,148
Music	329	384	306	346	1,365
Euclid	56	159	139	112	466
Algebra	49	121	31	38	239
Mensuration	206	156	241	92	695
Latin	2,674	3,339	1,796	1,153	8,962
Needlework					

This Inspection Report table reveals details of the units that made up school subjects in the early 1870s[54]

Faults upon inspection were matters such as *"indistinct and rapid articulation"* in reading; progress in arithmetic confined only to simple rules; indifferent mental arithmetic; poor grammatical composition of sentences; failure to exercise the children's powers of observation and comparison in Object Lessons; ineffective instruction in Drawing and Vocal Music.

Inspectors were also required to report on the status of school buildings, school dimensions, the number of classes and general conditions. They were interested in student regularity and punctuality, and the general behaviour of pupils. Accurate and timely attendance returns were of particular interest and loom large in the misdemeanors for which teachers could be disciplined. Such nebulous terms as *"mental effort"* and *"mental culture"* were also assessed as was the general proficiency of each class.

---

54   Ibid, Kiama Family History Centre

Schools or Depts	Below Standard	Equal to Standard	Above Standard	Total
Public	77	134	62	373
Provisional	124	26	4	154
Half-Time	51	13	7	71
Denominational	141	73	13	227
Total	393	246	86	825

Report on condition of schools inspected 1871-72. During the relevant years, Arthur's Inspectors were Mr Dwyer, for the Newcastle district and Mr Jones, for the Armidale district.[55]

Glen William was a vested school and Arthur had been schoolmaster there for a year before his first inspection in December 1868. The roll call was smaller than Croobyar, with only 14 boys and 18 girls. Only 25 of these were present on the day of inspection. *"The material state of the schoolhouse is good,"* the inspector reported; *"…it is well furnished and supplied with material. The organization and technical discipline are satisfactory. The teaching is methodical but the results of the examinations unsatisfactory. The mental tone of the school is low, arising chiefly from irregular attendance. Local supervision is not exercised but one member of the school board was present at the examination."*[56]

From this description we can suppose that this situation was not an improvement on Arthur's former school. Low attendance would prove to be the blight of this posting, with sectarian differences and local disasters conspiring to defeat his efforts to build up the school.

A further inspection took place in June 1869. At this time there were more students enrolled (39) but only 19 present at inspection. The ordinary average was 28. Once again the schoolhouse received commendation. *"(It) is in good condition, is commodious and has proper appointments. The*

---

55   ibid, State Records, Western Sydney Records Centre, Kingswood NSW

56   Ibid, State Records, Western Sydney Records Centre, Kingswood NSW

organization is correct, the pupils clean and orderly but are much wanting in energy. One very great hindrance to their progress is their irregularity of attendance. The instruction gives results which range from moderate to very fair."[57]

In view of the irregular attendance, this last comment indicates a high level of achievement for the schoolmaster. This is especially so when we consider that a new child had joined the family, with the birth of Albert Roberts on 19.06.1868.[58] Based on his death certificate (which listed him as an "invalid") and a reference to his disability in a letter of 1875, we can surmise that Albert had a serious disability, possibly cerebral palsy, or *'cerebral paralysis'* as it was referred to in that era. There is one photograph in existence (taken before his early death at 16 years 11 months) which shows him as a youth, seated in a wheelchair. In this he has the atrophied muscles and slender physique of someone with a long term disability.

The photograph is grainy but this well-dressed, well-cared for young man presents a much more cogent figure than that portrayed in references to him as *"a helpless idiot"* in 1875.[59] Doubtless, this brutal wording says more about the prevailing ignorance in that period regarding serious disabilities than it does about Albert himself. Cerebral palsy was only defined as a medical term in 1860 and, if the sufferer was fortunate, greeted with stoic acceptance by their immediate family. Arthur Roberts is listed as 31 on Albert's birth certificate while Elizabeth is listed as 27. In reality, this young couple were both less than 30 and responsible for three other active children. Now they had a child with serious incapacities, making their path much harder. A year later, on 29.09.1870, a further son, Ernest, was born.[60]

---

[57]   ibid, State Records, Western Sydney Records Centre, Kingswood NSW

[58]   Glen William near Clarence Town; Birth registration number 8298

[59]   Reference Number Item and Title 2/9280 8761, State Records, Western Sydney Records Centre, Kingswood NSW

[60]   Clarence Town; birth registration number 8661

Albert would have been a child of two when Glen William was visited again in September 1870, with the inspector noting a roll call of 38, and 31 students present at inspection. This was a definite improvement. However, the condition of the building was declining and repairs were needed. Furniture and working materials were now described as *"insufficient and inferior. There is no playground and as regards out offices, there is one closet in a wretched state. The organization, discipline and instruction are fairly effective. The local supervision is said to be satisfactory but no member of the Board was present at the examination."*[61]

What had happened to the furniture and materials in the previous two years? In 1868 the school was *"well furnished and supplied with materials"*. Now they were *"insufficient and inferior."* Part of the answer must lie in the increased roll-call.

Arthur Roberts stayed at Glen William until December 1871, a period of four years. Ms Burns-Woods' history of the school notes that this was longer than any previous teacher and that *"He did his best to raise attendances and make Glen William a flourishing school ..."* Sadly, she noted that eventually, Roberts had to admit defeat. Based on her analysis, sectarian divisions were at the root of the small and irregular attendances. For example, the Johnsons, a family of five children, were forced to withdraw in 1868 because the parish priest put pressure on their mother.

"The Roman Catholic clergy had always been opposed to the non-religious education," writes Ms Burns-Wood, *"but in the 1860s they began to exert strong pressure on parents to remove their children from Public Schools. The Bishop of Maitland was particularly firm in his instructions and in 1869 he ordered Roman Catholic parents to remove their children from Public Schools or to be refused the sacraments."*

Nature and economic hardship contributed to the decline of the school, with government archives citing a letter from Arthur Roberts (to the Council of Education in 1869) noting he could not secure an average

---

[61]   School Files, State Records, Western Sydney Records Centre, Kingswood NSW

attendance of 30. *"The Johnson children had temporarily returned so every child within three miles was attending the school. But the teacher said that 14 children had left the district and many lived on the opposite side of the river and were frequently kept away by floods, and the area was so poor that the children were often kept home to assist their parents"* (J. Burns-Woods).

By 1871 the attendance was down to 22. *"Mr Roberts explained that some farms in the area were untenanted and that the farmers on the Glen William estate had received notice to leave at the end of the year and had kept their children hard at work to secure a big crop before their lease expired. He also sent the Council a map of the area and a summary of each family. Finally in November 1871 when his salary was reduced because of the low attendance, poor Mr Roberts asked to be transferred, pointing out that it was no fault of his that the population of the area had decreased"*(J. Burns-Woods). Arthur's request was granted and, by 1873, Glen William had become a half-time school.

Arthur's transfer was essential. The family now consisted of five children less than 10 years old, one with a serious disability. His schoolmaster's salary was geared to the size and relative importance of his school. Figures from Council of Education Reports for 1871-72 reveal a newly implemented sliding scale in salaries, dependent on the number of pupils.[62]

| For an attendance below 25 but not below 20 .... £48 per annum |
| below 20 but not below 15 .... £36 per annum |
| below 15 but not below 12 .... £24 per annum |
| |
| If the attendances fall below 12, no salary to be paid |

The ordinary classification for teachers' salaries only applied where an average daily attendance of more than 30 scholars was maintained. According to the Council *"the cost of education in many schools was nearly double the amount that would have been required had a proper attendance*

---

[62]   Extract Report of Council of Education Upon   the Condition of Public Schools, Kiama Family History Centre

been maintained."[63] These provisions were only introduced in 1871-72 but it showed the extent to which the Roberts' family's prospects depended on Arthur maintaining student numbers.

Of course, school fees were meant to supplement the Council's salary and act as an inducement to the active recruitment of scholars. However, in some of the poorer communities, particularly in difficult times, scholars were absent and school fees went unpaid, a fact which the Council recognized was hardly the schoolmaster's fault. *"Exemptions have been granted when the low attendance was distinctly traceable to sickness, floods or excessive rains, or harvesting operations,"* they wrote.[64] Schoolmasters such as Arthur Roberts, who had a growing family to provide for, were especially disadvantaged by these situations.

To THE SECRETARY, COUNCIL OF EDUCATION,

SIR,

I beg to make application for a grant of the articles enumerated in the accompanying list, for the use of the _Public_ School at _Inverell_ in accordance with the above stated conditions, which I hereby engage to observe. The supply granted may be forwarded per _Steamer, Railway and both coach_. to the undersigned.

(Date) 2nd November 1872

Secretary.

A.R.Roberts.

Teacher.

(Date) 16. 11. 72

Examined and approved,

J. S. Jones

Inspector.

---

63   Ibid, Kiama Family History Centre

64   Ibid, Kiama Family History Centre

Hop Picking, Kent, early 1860s (top). Oast Houses, East Farleigh.

Elizabeth Roberts (nee Houston).

Arthur Robert Roberts.

Glen William School (top), and the town of Walcha in the 1870s.

Arthur William Henry Roberts, was pupil teacher at Scone Public School, working with his father AR Roberts. The family interest in cricket continued with Arthur William, who as headmaster at Smith Street Public School, Balmain, discovered a 15 year old batting prodigy, Archie Jackson who scored a century on debut for Australia v England.

Sparkes Creek (top) and the strange trees of Junction Creek.

English writer, Havelock Ellis, who taught at the village schools of Sparkes and Junction Creeks, working to his headmaster, AR Roberts – the "Humbug" of Kanga Creek.

Arthur Roberts and family at Louth, 1882 (top)
and Maggie Roberts, born 1864, died in 1893.

Walcha 1872

The family's next move was further north, to the small town of Walcha in the Armidale district, where a national school had been established in the late 1850s. Arthur's time there coincided with Victoria's introduction of an education bill setting up a department of public instruction, which abolished government aid to denominational schools. Advocates for free, compulsory and secular education in New South Wales urged the adoption of similar legislation here and although this did not take place for a further eight years, the relationship between church and state was shifting. Conflict with the Roman Catholic Church was particularly intense, a factor that proved fatal to enrolment numbers at Walcha.

In her study of education in Walcha, Heather Murchie records that the site for Walcha Public School was a 2 acre block on the corner of Fitzroy and Middle Streets.[65] As expected, locals paid a third of the cost and the school opened with an initial enrolment of 40 students in June 1859. School fees were set at 20 shillings/quarter.

However, within a few short years, enrolment had virtually halved with only 21 students attending. Reasoning that high school fees may have been prohibitive for many people, these were reduced in 1862. First Class pupils paid 8 shillings, Second Class pupils, 12 shillings and pupils attending Third Class and higher paid 15 shillings/quarter. Apparently these reductions did little to help because attendance was still low in 1864. Disheartened, members of the local board resigned while the resident teacher applied for a transfer on account of his wife's ill health.

The school must have been inoperative for a period as revealed in a letter of January 1872 before Arthur's arrival. In this, the Public School Board implored the Council to send a good teacher as their children were *"roaming the bush"* and *"growing up in ignorance"*.[66] Further correspon-

---

65   Centenary of Education Supplement, The Walena News, 10 September 1959

66   Education Department Archive, School Files, State Records, Western Sydney Records Centre, Kingswood NSW

dence from Mr Jones, the local Inspector, gave the pleasing news that Arthur Robert Roberts would start work on 22 January 1872. A few days later the Walcha correspondent for *The Armidale Express* recorded:

"On Tuesday last Mr Arthur Roberts, late of Glen William, opened our Public School. At present he has but a poor attendance, but no doubt, with a little exertion on his part, he will bring up the numbers to a standard of 30 to 40 children."

The costs of the Roberts family's relocation are listed in a letter to William Wilkins soon after their arrival. The hire of two horses and a dray to transport family and belongings was £15, with tolls and punt a further 12/6. *"I beg to inform the Council that the journey cost me nearly twice as much as the amount above named,"* Arthur wrote. A note at the bottom reveals that payment of the requested costs was originally *"Deferred"* before £15 was granted.[67]

In February the schoolmaster informed Wilkins that he had opened the school on 23 January with only 4 boys and 3 girls but that *"I have now enrolled 17 boys and 12 girls and believe I shall be able to average 30 by the end of the present month, February."* That same month he sent a request for materials and equipment. *"The supplies requested,"* he continued, *"may be forwarded by Steamer, rail Cobb Express to Uralla and Mail to Walcha."*[68]

The requisition order for materials for the Walcha Public School is dated 15 March 1872.[69] Supplied were granted in relation to numbers of children enrolled. Since they remained the property of the Council, it was important for school teachers to keep them in good order and ensure they were not removed from the premises. Equipment was often requisitioned in the dozens and included slates, slate pencils, pencil cases, pens, pen holders, ink and ink powders. A variety of maps was required, including

---

67   Reference Number Item and Title 2/9280 8761, State Records, Western Sydney Records Centre, Kingswood NSW

68   Ibid, State Records, Western Sydney Records Centre, Kingswood NSW

69   Ibid, State Records, Western Sydney Records Centre, Kingswood NSW

maps of Europe, Asia, Africa, North and South America, Australia, New South Wales, Palestine, England, Ireland, Scotland and the British Isles. A blackboard, inkwells, easels and diagrams were necessities, as well as a zoological chart. The necessary library – all in multiples from 10-40 - included scripture books, reading books, Australian Class Books and Lesson Books in various grades, and reading lessons in sheets. A clock, desks, tables and forms were also essential.

The extensive correspondence from this placement gives us detailed information into the family's financial affairs. A memo of 17 February from the accountant for the Council of Education notes that Arthur was to receive an annual salary of £120, to take effect on 1 January 1872. However, the late starting date of the placement was to cause conflict with the Council who felt the schoolmaster should not receive pay for the first three weeks of the year. A letter from Arthur dated 26 February attempts to clarify this, with the explanation that his appointment had started on the first day of the year. At the bottom, there is a terse note from the Council; *"Inform of the extremely unsatisfactory nature of this reply."*[70]

Arthur sent a further letter of clarification on 8 March.

"I received my letter of appointment to this school on Saturday night, 30ᵗʰ December, 1871," he writes. *"I immediately prepared to sell off my furniture as it was impossible to bring it here, a distance of 268 miles. We started Monday 8ᵗʰ January and arrived here Saturday night, 20ᵗʰ January, after dark, travelling the whole time, even on Sunday.*

As the week ending 6ᵗʰ January was included in the Christmas holidays and as I felt certain the Council of Education knew that I could not arrive here sooner than I did; also it being mentioned in my letter of appointment that my salary was to commence on 1ˢᵗ January 1872, instead of from the date I took charge of this school, I concluded that the Council intended to pay me for the whole month as I was actually at work during the whole time, although not teaching the whole time.

---

[70]   ibid, State Records, Western Sydney Records Centre, Kingswood NSW

I am sorry if I have made a mistake and request the Council of Education to pay me what they think I deserve for the month of January.

Apologizing for giving you so much trouble"[71]

This letter was apparently successful as he did receive salary from the original starting date but it is difficult not to sympathize with his plight or to conclude that these struggles took a personal toll on his confidence and his good faith with his employer.

By June the focus of attention had shifted to the need for repairs to the school. The Council was agreeable but only if the local Public School Board paid one third of the costs. The Board refused to comply. For his part, Secretary Wilkins requested a detailed account of the Walcha buildings for the previous five years. These were forthcoming, including repairs to the teacher's residence, no doubt necessary with the birth of another daughter, Elizabeth, on 29.08.1872.[72]

A column from the Walcha correspondent in *The Armidale Express* dated 28 August 1872 noted that the school had just received a visit from Mr Jones, Inspector of Public Schools. After examining the children, the correspondent reported, *"He was well satisfied with the progress they had made during the last eight or nine months under the tuition of Mr Roberts. The number on the roll exceeds 60, the highest number ever attained before since the establishment of the school. It is alike satisfactory to the master and the parents of the children that they are being trained in the way they should go."* Imagine their bewilderment when, a few short months later, the Council of Education recommended Arthur's removal to the much larger centre of Inverell. The Walcha correspondent for *The Armidale Express* took up the matter in his column, dated 9 October 1872.

"The inhabitants of this town are highly indignant at the conduct of the Inspector of Schools in taking away so unceremoniously our Teacher,

---

[71]   Reference Number Item and Title 2/9280 8761, State Records, Western Sydney Records Centre, Kingswood NSW

[72]   Armidale; birth registration number 5991

Mr Roberts, and removing him to Inverell, as though we were not entitled to a good Teacher as well as any other district. We have long felt the want of a good man, and Mr Roberts for the short time he was here had won the esteem of all the parents by the way in which he brought the children on. But all of a sudden the school is closed, and the children are running about in all directions. It is to be hoped that the gentlemen forming the Local Board will see further into the matter and clear themselves of any want of attention to the study of our rising generation."

Apparently unable to alter the situation, the whole Public School Board sent letters of resignation to the Council.[73] The schoolmaster had built up an average attendance of 40 to 50 pupils and in the process raised returns from school fees. Nonetheless, notice of his removal was posted on 28 September with one week's provision for his removal to the new placement. The Council had also decided to delay any repairs to the Walcha school until a new teacher was appointed.

Leaving the key to the school with Mr Kelly, Secretary of the School Board, Arthur and Elizabeth Roberts and their six children (one a babe in arms) left Walcha on 7 October 1872. The schoolmaster had been there eight and a half months. With no immediate replacement for him, the school was forced to close. The Secretary of the local Public School Board wrote a strongly worded letter to the Council, protesting at these developments.

"The Board feel that so far as the removal of the teacher is concerned the Council of Education have not treated them with that courtesy they are entitled to, and they wish to record it ... has caused much bitterness of feeling amongst the parents of pupils and done great injury to the cause of public education in Walcha."[74]

---

[73]   Education Department Archive, School Files, State Records, Western Sydney Records Centre, Kingswood NSW

[74]   ibid, State Records, Western Sydney Records Centre, Kingswood NSW

Walcha was not the only school to find itself bereft of a schoolmaster. The training system for teachers was coming under scrutiny in these years because it failed to adapt teachers for smaller country schools, whether public, denominational, provisional and half-time. Council of Education records show that around forty such schools were vacant early in 1873, with an urgent need for teachers to fill the vacancies.

"Even when persons applied for such situations it was frequently found that their knowledge of the colony was limited to Sydney and its vicinity … When trained teachers are appointed to these situations the evil is aggravated, for such Teachers naturally expect higher emoluments and greater consideration than the circumstances of the locality could afford."[75]

Residents of country districts were considered suitable but alas, suitable candidates for the position of pupil teacher in these areas were often lacking.

We do not know Arthur's feelings about the transfer but it seems safe to assume that if he knew what awaited him in Inverell, he would have looked upon this short period at Walcha as the calm before the storm.

Inverell 1872

Arthur Robert Roberts *"entered upon his duties"* at the new school on 14 October 1872. There were 96 pupils on the roll. That November he received official confirmation that his salary would remain at £120 per annum, or £10 per month. He had received notice to leave Walcha on the first day of October and had packed up and left within the week, travelling in a dray with three horses at a cost of £15. Lodging for the family was a further £5.

As Elizabeth Wiedemann describes in *World of its own: Inverell's early years 1827-1920*, the town could attribute its growth to Colin Ross, who had first set up an inn on the MacIntyre River in December 1853 and

---

75   Extract from Report to the Council of Education Upon the Condition of Public Schools, Kiama Family History Centre

"raised (Inverell) from an obscure stock reserve to ... a postal centre ... a surveyed town and finally a municipality, all within 20 years."[76]

In early years the town centre was in Byron Street and it was here that the first national school opened in one large room. A second school was built on the corner of Campbell and Rivers Streets in 1863. The town's location on the MacIntyre River meant the streets were full of bog holes, some apparently big enough to drown in. *"The biggest (c.1m deep) was between Inverell Public School and the Swanbrook Road... wild ducks were found and shot (there) in abundance."* These pools created a public nuisance when they dried, becoming muddy and malodorous. A half metre of black mud was reputed to stick to your boots after a walk in the main streets in 1871. This same black mud caused havoc on roads leading to Inverell from every direction.[77]

The Free Selection Acts of 1861 had stimulated settlement in the district, interrupted only by a major flood in 1864. By 1866 it was a thriving centre of c.500 people. As such, the Public School was prey to the sectarian divisions of these years, particularly after a Roman Catholic School was opened in 1867. Parental expectations were not high, with Elizabeth Wiedemann reporting that most children in the district were at work on the farm by 8-9 years.[78] Elizabeth Hunter notes that a teacher's residence was built in September 1868 *"a weatherboard structure, built on sleepers and roofed with shingles – the kitchen a detached slab kitchen roofed with bark but not floored."*[79]

In mid 1871, the discovery of tin led to a speculative rush and an influx of hundreds of miners. It was possibly a factor in Arthur's transfer from

---

[76]   p54, World of its own: Inverell's early years 1827-1920, Elizabeth Wiedemann, Inverell Shire Council and Devill Publicity, Inverell 1981

[77]   ibid, Wiedemann, p68

[78]   ibid, Wiedemann, p76

[79]   Education Department, Schools Files Archive, State Records, Western Sydney Records Centre, Kingswood NSW

Walcha as school numbers must suddenly have erupted. The population fluctuated in these years, inflated by 1,500-2,000 extra people at any one time. In 1878, Wiedemann states that it was c.1000. *"The sudden rise was felt severely by the town's essential services,"* she noted. The initial rush led to high prices in busy stores and hotels filled to overflowing. These factors would aversely affect the new schoolmaster in his search for an assistant. *"At Inverell, the hotels were overcrowded 'two in a bed' being common."*[80]

As if these upheavals were not enough, on 21 December, within weeks of the Roberts family's arrival, Inverell experienced a devastating flood. Most of the town's buildings were inundated and several people drowned crossing swollen rivers and creeks. Locals speculated that 200mm of rain had fallen in one night and townspeople woke to ankle-deep water. By 3pm that day, when the flood waters began to fall, there was mud and debris everywhere. The disaster generated a building boom, part of which included new Chinese-run boarding houses. With so much activity taking place, wine shops and saloons also proliferated and advertisements touted *"brewed hop beer, ginger beer, champagne cider, cordials and vinegar"*.[81]

Apparently the first years of this period were *"ones of excitement and lawlessness,"* with the added element of racial unrest when an influx of Chinese *"tributers"* arrived to mine tin for a fixed wage.[82] With customary industry, many of these Chinese settlers went on to open market gardens, shops and boarding houses, generating ill feeling among some of the white settler community and accusations of gambling and other vices. Partly in response to these new 'evils' a local chapter of the Sons of Temperance was instituted in 1876 and we can presume that there was plenty of scope for their good works. However, this is to pre-empt the sad story of these few years and we must return to the end of 1872 to follow the progress of the Roberts family in this new posting.

---

[80]   ibid, Wiedemann p97-98

[81]   ibid, Wiedemann, p95

[82]   Ibid, Wiedemann p81

The parleying between schoolmaster and Council of Education in these first weeks reveals the prickly nature of their relationship. Arthur invoiced the Council for travelling expenses, which they paid, but there was less agreement over an invoice for a portion of his salary. Arthur had claimed £1.13.0 for five days work but the Council wanted to reduce this to £1.12.3. Roberts pointed out that by his calculations it was £1.12.10½ but that *"I believe any employer would have accepted the debt as £1.13.0."*[83] This sort of pettifogging approach clearly rankled with the schoolmaster who, at the Council's behest, had travelled more than 600 miles over the previous year. But like all bureaucracies before and since, the Council was not interested in special pleading. The growing system was still plagued with costly inefficiencies and they seemed determined to allow no quarter where money was concerned.

The Inverell Public School had been constructed before the discovery of tin in the area and as such, the building and its resources proved too small for the growing roll call of children. This was obvious to the schoolmaster soon after his arrival. That December he requisitioned new materials, furniture and fittings. Above all, he needed a competent assistant but this was proving hard to find. It may be that some found the character of the growing town unacceptable while others were put off by the spiraling costs for accommodation and services.

Arthur outlined the difficulties in a letter to William Wilkins in May 1873.[84] There were 127 scholars on the roll, he wrote, and an average attendance of 95. A Miss Hannigan had been appointed but had *"declined the situation."* As a result, and notwithstanding her young family, Elizabeth Roberts was forced to be at school all day, assisting her husband. Although many of the students were older, the new schoolmaster despaired of finding a pupil teacher within their ranks since they were *"far lower in*

---

83   Reference Number Item and Title 2/9280 8761, State Records, Western Sydney Records Centre, Kingswood NSW

84   Ibid, State Records, Western Sydney Records Centre, Kingswood NSW

point of knowledge than any others I have ever had anything to do with and consequently require more labour as many of them are old for school."

The Council acted quickly, appointing as Assistant Teacher, a Mr Robert Delow, late of St John's School, Parramatta. This gentleman's arrival and speedy departure created even more problems but fortunately for us, his correspondence with the Council of Education generated a wealth of detail about conditions in Inverell at the time. Arthur Roberts was informed of his appointment on 2 June 1873. Delow had been teaching at Parramatta, at that time one of the most settled and civilized districts in 19th century Australia. But here we must turn to Mr Delow to tell the story for himself, as recorded in a letter to the Council.[85]

"After due consideration of the position of assistant teacher to the Public School, Inverell, I have come to the decision to decline entering upon the duties of such and to return to Sydney by the coach today. I have carefully considered the emolument derivable therefrom and find such would not be better than my previous position while everything is much dearer than in Sydney. The accommodation offered at 20/- ... per week is scarcely fit to put a horse in comparatively speaking. The town I thoroughly dislike and these, together with other reasons of a private character, induce me to take the course mentioned."

We do not know the nature of these *"private reasons"* but the Council seems to have inferred they related to the character of Arthur Roberts, the schoolmaster who would work closely with Mr Delow. Roberts had reported Delow's hasty departure in a telegram, dated 25 June. *"Mr Delow arrived 23rd instant left today no reason given did not see the school."*[86]

The Council of Education was not impressed with the hapless Mr Delow and asked him to return the travelling expenses of £9.10.0 which

85   ibid, State Records, Western Sydney Records Centre, Kingswood NSW

86   ibid, State Records, Western Sydney Records Centre, Kingswood NSW

they had advanced. This led Delow to explain his reasons in more detail and excerpts from that letter appear below.

"I started from Sydney on Monday 16th June instant to enter upon my duties. Owing to bad weather which caused the steamer to be behind time in reaching Newcastle and to the fact that the coach only runs twice a week to Inverell, I was delayed four days on the road and only reached that town at 2pm on Monday 23rd instant. Shortly after arrival I made myself known to the master, Mr Roberts, who, in the course of conversation distinctly gave me to understand the fees pertaining to my position … an amount of £3 a month. During the evening of the same day, in company with Mr Roberts, I showed my official appointment to Mr Colin Ross and to Mr Mann, who desired to know when I intended to begin work. To this I replied, probably on the following day but was not certain as a little time was necessary to look around. Having made due inquiries respecting accommodation, etc, and having well considered all the circumstances connected with the position, I thought it best to decline entering upon duties, on the following grounds-

The emoluments derivable from the position would not quite equal those obtained from my late position.

Everything in Inverell is from 75 to 100 per cent dearer than in Sydney; an example of which is given in the fact that washing, which in Sydney costs from 2/6 to 3/- per dozen, costs in Inverell from 4/6 to 5/- per dozen.

Accommodation with any claim to respectability was not to be had in town under from twenty five to thirty shillings a week. Apart from Public Houses, at which permanent quarters could not be obtained under £2 5s per week, there was but one place where accommodation could be had and that of a wretched character at the terms first named.

Viewing all these circumstances the position was not to all appearances in any way an improvement upon my last; and this taken in conjunction with the fact that I have now been nearly nine years in the Council's service, induced me to return. Having come to the decision and notified the same by letter to Mr Roberts I left Inverell at half past ten on the morning of Wednesday 25th June instant, and arrived in Sydney at five o'clock in the afternoon of Saturday, 28th June instant.

I have, therefore, respectfully to request the Council to cancel the appointment; and although I have been under great expense ... in proceeding to Inverell and to loss of time, I am prepared should the Council desire it, to refund the amount allowed me for travelling expenses."[87]

Mr Delow refunded the money to the Council and in August expressed his regret at the decision not to refuse the Inverell appointment. The Council had apparently informed him that, given his behaviour, they were not interested in appointing him to another posting.

"It is with regret I view the course pursued by me in connection to the appointment to Inverell Public School and have respectfully to request the Council to overlook it, as it was caused partly through ignorance of the consequences such a step would entail and partly through not duly considering my duty to the Council." This appeal was successful for the Council marked it *"eligible for further employment".*[88]

Their response may have been due to the need for trained teachers rather than any leniency on their part. They expected teachers to undertake whatever posting they determined and prove themselves worthy participants of the growing national system of education. By our standards, they also seem to have expected a certain 'kow-towing' to their authority which rankled with some of the schoolmasters who had arrived here from England and for that matter, with some of their local counterparts.

Winter found Inverell Public School still without an assistant but with a larger roll call. With its low ceiling and cramped conditions, the school was suffocatingly hot in summer. As a result, many parents kept children away until the cooler months. The cooler weather caused other practical problems, with Arthur requesting coal supplies for the school. There was

---

87   ibid, State Records, Western Sydney Records Centre, Kingswood NSW

88   ibid, State Records, Western Sydney Records Centre, Kingswood NSW

an urgent need for a bigger school building, as outlined by Colin Ross, a prominent member of the local Public School Board.

"I am directed to inform you that at the last meeting of the local board it was decided that a new school house is absolutely necessary and that steps be taken for the erection of a building to accommodate 250 pupils.

The present building is now quite unsuitable for the town and the climate. The ceilings are so low and the room so crowded that in summertime it is almost suffocating and must be unhealthy.

I beg to enclose a plan suggested by the board, the walls to be brick on stone foundation; twelve feet clear to wall plates – open ceiling to secure plenty of ventilation – the estimated cost being £600. The present schoolroom could be fitted for boarders.

Public School Board to be furnished with copy of architect's report.

I am also requested to again bring your attention to the want of an assistant teacher. You will of course observe in teacher's abstract the number of scholars on the roll and the average attendance.

Mr Ross, Honorary Secretary"[89]

The appeal for a new assistant was successful and that August, Arthur was informed of the appointment of Mr John Anderson, who held a 111A teaching classification. Anderson would receive an annual salary of £60 and a share of school fees.[90] With this in mind, Arthur wrote to the Council of Education that September, applying for a promotion under Article 39 of their regulations and explaining that the assistant's arrival would considerably reduce his own salary.

"I have held my present grade Class 11 Section A over ten years," he wrote, *"and should not have troubled the Council now had not food and clothing been so excessively high here as to render a reduction of one third from the fees a very serious consideration in a large family."*[91]

---

[89] ibid, State Records, Western Sydney Records Centre, Kingswood NSW

[90] This is considerably more than the £36 annual salary mentioned by Mr Delow

[91] ibid, State Records, Western Sydney Records Centre, Kingswood NSW

At the base of this letter, with no reason given, William Wilkins has written *"Declined"*. The rationale for the decision was more forthcoming in the Examiner's Report, dated 13.09.1873, on Arthur Roberts' request for promotion to Class 1 Section B. [92]

"Mr Roberts has no valid claim on the Council for the following reasons.

For years past his results have barely reached the average "Fair" and have as a rule been considerably below standard requirements.

He has little energy, seldom teaches thoroughly or impressively and rarely succeeds in any school. Such was the case for years at Glen William and Croobyar.

Between the years 1865 and 1870, he was accused of frequenting taverns and appears to have exceeded the bounds of temperance.

Mr Roberts has had two new schools since 1871 and we have no intimation of any particular success either at Walcha or Inverell. His low results, want of energy and general deficiency in the qualifications of sound teachers render promotion to Class 1 entirely out of the question"

An earlier undated report by the Inspector for the Newcastle District also made mention of the schoolmaster's *"failing."*[93]

"During my stay at Clarence Town and at my visit to Glen William I heard of nothing detrimental to the teacher's character. I had conversations with two of the Public School Board, Messrs, A McFarlane and W. Johnston and neither of those gentlemen informed me of the failing to which you allude. Thus the statement respecting his moral influence was so far as I knew bona fide."

These implications are worth examining in detail. The debts that followed Roberts from Ulladulla and led to his insolvency must have created a bad impression but the claim that he had *"little energy"* is contradicted by reports from some of the communities where he worked. His arrival in Inverell had been preceded by a report from Walcha that he was *"appar-*

---

92   ibid, State Records, Western Sydney Records Centre, Kingswood NSW

93   ibid, State Records, Western Sydney Records Centre, Kingswood NSW

ently an energetic teacher."[94] Moreover, the success or failure of struggling country schools can hardly be blamed on the schoolmaster alone, especially in places like Inverell, where the town was going through a boom period. However, the charge of *"frequenting taverns … and … exceeding the bounds of temperance"* is hard to dispute. Schoolmasters were watched over, first by local patrons and later by local Public School Boards and it could be that some of these had reported unfavourably on Arthur's drinking habits.

He had grown up in a society where hop-brewed beer was healthier and freer from disease that drinking water and in an era when beer was widely used for nutritional purposes, as a food and a dietary supplement. Alcohol also had medicinal applications - as *"a sure-acting stimulant and analgesic in both hospital and private practice"*.[95] These perceptions were gradually changing but in the 1870s many facts that we now take for granted were only just emerging.

It is also worth noting that colonial alcohol trading was largely unregulated and local brews often contained 5-6% more alcohol than British beers. Australian wines were reputed to contain 50% more alcohol than French wines.[96] Their ingredients were toxic, with salicylic acid causing gastric irritation and other ingredients causing delirium and in some cases, death. The case for local spirituous liquors was no better and alcohol came to be regarded as a leading cause of insanity, with sufferers

---

[94]   ibid, State Records, Western Sydney Records Centre, Kingswood NSW

[95]   Curing Alcoholism in Australia, 1880s-1920s, F.B. Smith, Australian National University

[96]   State Records, Western Sydney Records Centre, Kingswood NSW

confined in asylums for treatment.[97] Meanwhile *"all ministries depended heavily on drink revenues"*.[98] All these circumstances may have been factors in Arthur's individual decline but decline it was and within a decade of these events in his life, medical researchers would recast alcohol as a toxin rather than a tonic.

The signature on the Council of Education document is obscured but it does not appear to be that of William Wilkins. If it is that of the local district inspector, Mr Jones, then the report reveals a marked decline in his opinion of the schoolmaster since Jones had reported favourably on Roberts at Glen William. The growth in Arthur's family, the need to re-establish themselves in one town after another, the practical problems of Inverell and Roberts' age may all have been factors.

He was now a man of 32 and had been away from his homeland for 13 incident-packed years. Natural disaster, lumpen students, suffocating heat and practical difficulties had collided with a certain 'wild west' period in Inverell's history. The alcohol flowed freely in its many hotels and taverns and we can speculate that what had been a habit of regular drinking now tipped the scales to frequent drunkenness.

Robert's request for promotion had been submitted alongside repeated requests for a new school building but in spite of the Council's in principle support and the arrival of the long-awaited assistant teacher, conditions at Inverell Public continued to cause heartache and frustration. The situation was so bad at the end of 1873 that two new forms were requested because

---

[97]   The story of Arthur's oldest brother, David Roberts is relevant here. On 7 May 1887 the Sydney Morning Herald carried a report of his death referred to him as "a very intemperate man." They noted he had been in the 'Receiving House' three times within the previous 12 months "from the effects of excessive drinking and that in the days preceding his death he had "barely kept down food, took sleeping draughts … (and) died of syncope, consequent on the excessive use of alcohol."

[98]   Ibid, Smith, Australian National University

many children had to stand.[99] It was feared that some of the children would leave if this situation continued.

The struggle for approval to build a new school was in the foreground during these years. On behalf of the local Board, Colin Ross guaranteed a sum of £200 and requested the Council of Education to provide *"a rough plan of a building that could be completed for the limit contemplated that they may report or suggest on it. The Board would be glad to see a building erected which could be extended hereafter."*[100]

Full plans and specifications were sent that October and, with some modifications, approved.

At long last, as reported in a history of Inverell Public School in *The Tide of Time*, the new school building was approved and the contract won by Mr Witham for £800.[101] But work was again delayed and when a further year passed, Mr Witham declined the job. The building was finally begun in 1875 and built for a cost of £1,085 by William Pender and Samuel Coulten. By this time, Arthur Robert Roberts was no longer the schoolmaster of Inverell Public School. A regular inspection of 8-9 July 1875 had found serious flaws in his teaching and management of the school. From the high figure cited in 1872-73, the enrolment had fallen to 84, with 76 pupils present at the inspection.

"The schoolroom is too small for the requirements of the place," wrote Mr Jones, *"but steps are in progress for the erection of new and more commodious premises. Present buildings in fair repair and well kept and garden and other surroundings creditable to the teacher. There is still no 4th class in the school and its absence together with the comparatively low results reached in all but 2nd class under the assistant teacher reflect great discredit on the teacher. The reading throughout the school is very unsatisfactory and there is evidence of a*

99   Reference Number Item and Title 2/9280 8761, State Records, Western Sydney Records Centre, Kingswood NSW

100   ibid, State Records, Western Sydney Records Centre, Kingswood NSW

101   Tide of Time, Inverell 1872-73, p23

want of thoroughness in the teaching and an absence of proper mental train-
ing. The average proficiency of the pupils is about 'tolerable' – the attainments
in 3rd class being much below the requirements of the 'standard'."[102]

The effects of these comments on the schoolmaster's morale can only be guessed but reports of his spirits, depressed by the effects of intoxication, reached the Council and on 30 September 1875 he was dismissed.

Some of the townspeople rallied in his support, presenting a public petition asking the Council to rescind their decision. They praised Roberts' work and efforts to improve the school and his establishment of two choirs and a brass band. Mention was also made of the needs of his large family. Another child, Harold, had been born that January, meaning they were now a family of two adults and seven children.[103] These efforts by the local community were partially successful. The Council of Education decided that instead of outright dismissal, Roberts' classification would be demoted from 11A to 11B and he would be moved to a new posting at his own expense. The move took place and the following January Arthur Roberts took up his new post as schoolmaster at Scone.

---

[102]   State Records, Western Sydney Records Centre, Kingswood NSW

[103]   31 January 1875; Inverell birth registration number 12873

Scone

Once again the family had to undertake a strenuous journey of over 187 miles with their seven children – one disabled and one still a babe in arms. Before these epic journeys, they often sold off household furnishings to reduce transport costs.[104] Their destination, Scone, was a more established environment than many of their previous postings.

As early as 1863 the inhabitants of the town had been reported as *"of a settled character likely to support the school if a good teacher is sent."*[105] At that time there were upwards of 200 children in the area, with 70 then enrolled at the local denominational school. Application for a non-vested national school was made that year, with more than 30 pupils expected to enroll. The character of the local clergyman would be crucial to its success and the Board of Education anticipated his opposition. Local patrons were drawn from a range of occupations, including publican, pound keeper, storekeeper, farmer and Clerk of Petty Sessions.[106]

The school was duly established but attendance waxed and waned over the following decade. It was reasoned that a proper school building would improve attendances but the situation continued and poor inspection reports led to the school closing for a brief period late in 1872 or early 1873.[107] In 1874, local enthusiasts banded together to lobby for a *"worthy"* school for the town and that year they canvassed for suitable sites.[108] James Little, Honorary Secretary of the new Public School Board, wrote to the Council of Education of these developments, promising the board would

---

104   ibid, State Records, Western Sydney Records Centre, Kingswood NSW

105   The History of Scone Public School, 'Laurae', Scone Public School, Its Genesis and History, Interesting Data, Scone Advocate, 27 August 1927, p10

106   State Records, Western Sydney Records Centre, Kingswood NSW

107   State Records, Western Sydney Records Centre, Kingswood NSW

108   State Records, Western Sydney Records Centre, Kingswood NSW

contribute £400 towards the erection of a building.[109] A list of impressive local names was included, among them, Dr John Creed, a noted physician who was later to 'cross swords' with Arthur Roberts. The district inspector, Mr Jones, remained the same.

The building of the new school was still in progress when the Roberts family arrived so Arthur's first teaching post was at St Luke's, a local Church of England school. [110] This augured well for the relationship between church and state. In fact, the clergyman, the Reverend John Shaw proved to be a consistent ally and, in line with government policy, gave classes in religious instruction at the school. Shaw was an enlightened man, who wrote for the Newcastle Herald and was a supporter of Aboriginal causes in the district.[111]

By July, the school was finished and Arthur Roberts and his charges made the move to the new building. At the same time, and with the minister's agreement, the church school closed down. By the time the inspector visited in mid November, there were 117 pupils on the roll. Apparently the schoolmaster had profited by the disastrous end to his Inverell posting because the present course of instruction was reported to be complete and well regulated, with good punctuality, character, discipline and efficiency. For their part, the pupils were reported to be from average proficiency to *"very fair."*[112]

---

[109]   The application was approved in June 1874 and the building completed in 1876 at a cost of £1,250. In the event, the local community's contribution was to purchase the site, with the whole cost of the building borne by the Council.

[110]   Erected by Thomas Hudson, contractor

[111]   'Margaret of the Awakabal', Vicki Grieves, University of Newcastle

[112]   Scone Public School, Its Genesis and History, Interesting Data, Scone Advocate, 27 August 1927

The Maitland Mercury & Hunter River General Advertiser carried a lengthy overview of the state of Scone's public school in 1876.[113]

"(It is) a very nice building for a public school … an excellent sample of those school buildings which, thanks to the Public Schools Act and the liberality of the Parliament, occupy a prominent position in so many of our country towns … The country that possesses, in every principal town and village, a specimen of the trim, neat school building which the Council erects when the importance of the locality and the funds available demand it, is in a fair way of advancement. The Scone Public School fronts Liverpool Street; it is built upon a square allotment of two acres in extent – a noble playground; - and it has accommodation for one hundred and eighty children. That is rather more than enough for the present demand; but the attendance will, it is hoped, soon increase. As we believe, the establishment of the school is an instance of the operation killing-out (sic) a thriving denominational school, to the benefit of the children of the town; the disposition in the case being that the former supporters of the denominational school are willing, in the presence of public necessities, that it should give up the ghost. The Public School and the Church of England School might co-exist but they would compete too closely, and the Church of England School would be cheerfully given up, in order that the teaching power may be strengthened and consolidated.

The newspaper also carried details of the schoolmaster's house.

"The master's house is well advanced towards completion and a well is being sunk on the premises for the use of the children and the master. There are only three living rooms … a defect which might have been cured if there were a separate kitchen built. It is rather too bad, on many grounds, that the kitchen of a school master should lessen his house room, by taking up one apartment altogether, and the cost of building a separate kitchen would have

---

[113] 'Other Scone Matters' Maitland Mercury & Hunter River General Advertiser (NSW 1843-1893), Thursday 9 March 1876

been trifling. The whole building, which is of brick roofed with shingles, is creditable to the contractor, Mr John Hudson, of Scone. "[114]

The schoolmaster also came in for mention. *The Mercury* reported that Mr Roberts had been described as:

"... an excellent teacher and a good disciplinarian. The character of his role may be gathered from the portraiture of a young gentleman, whose opinion was that though Mr Roberts was sharp, he was always sharp-uniformly strict, so that you knew the ground you stood upon with him, and sought always to keep up to the mark. You were never induced to be lax in study in the hope that the master would have a careless fit. That does strike us as very excellent, healthy and beneficial discipline, and we can understand the desire of the Scone people to have Mr Roberts' services over a larger area of educational ground. "[115]

The Roberts family spent six years at Scone, with two more children born during this period – Victoria in 1878 and Ambrose in 1880.[116] Arthur was, at the time, a man in his prime; 36 years old at the beginning of the posting and 42 at the end. His obituary stated that *"while stationed at Scone Mr Roberts was correspondent for the Mercury."*[117] We have no way of knowing the exact dates for this journalistic role or even if he wrote each and every column with the Scone correspondent's by-line during this period. There are between 300 and 400 columns, many lengthy. It is thus a tantalizing prospect to read these in detail to make what we can of the character and personality of the writer.[118]

For the purposes of this story we will consider only reports that mention the school and/or Arthur Roberts; or which, by inference, can

---

[114] Arthur Roberts' request for a kitchen and wash house for the teacher's residence was granted and the new rooms were built by November 1876

[115] Ibid, The Maitland Mercury & Hunter River General Advertiser

[116] Scone birth registration numbers 21884 and 24162 respectively

[117] The Maitland Daily Mercury, 22 February 1898

[118] A selection of these columns can be found at trove.nla.gov.au

probably be attributed to him. If little else, these accounts suggest the tenor of his life during this period and give insight into the way he may have spent some of his leisure time. In his first years at Scone, the School of Arts came in for frequent mention and since his name is occasionally linked with that, there will also be some attention to it and the role it played in the community.

The first mention of Arthur is in connection with his appointment as teacher of *"our long wished-for Public School."*[119] A further recount of 11 October provided a wealth of colourful detail and suggested a cordial relationship implied between teacher and ministers. [120]

"On Saturday last, 7th, the Rev, John Shaw B.A. incumbent of this district, invited the members of the church choir, the Sunday School teacher and the children attending the religious instruction class at the Public School to an excursion by rail to Aberdeen. The company, numbering about 70, left Scone by the 7:45 morning train and arrived on the ground at 8:30 o'clock when various amusements were heartily entered into. The Rev D.D. Rutledge and Mr A. Roberts, the teacher of the Public School, materially contributed to the enjoyment of the little ones. At eleven o'clock the company sat down to an excellent luncheon consisting of poultry, ham and beef, followed by cakes, tarts, jam sandwiches and other delicacies, with a dessert in the shape of oranges and lollies, there being also an abundance of excellent tea. Refreshment was again provided at 2pm. The sun was hot but a cool breeze was blowing all day. The excursionists returned to Scone at 3:30pm after having enjoyed themselves immensely, through the kind liberality of Rev J Shaw who must have been pleased to see so many happy and pleasant faces around him."

This impression is reinforced by a report of a Sunday School Feast at St Luke's the following month, at which 280 children were present.[121]

---

[119]   The Maitland Mercury & Hunter River General Advertiser, 20 July 1876

[120]   Ibid, 14 October 1876

[121]   Ibid, 14 November 1876

"Mr Roberts marshaled the children in a way that shows they are under the care of an earnest and efficient teacher. Scone is one of the few places in the colony where the Public School has been accepted by the Church of England, in the hope that his constant attention to the religious instruction of the children may counteract any results arising from the failure of the Denominational School. Hitherto the experiment must be pronounced a success. The good order and demeanour of the children were most marked. Their school songs were very pleasingly sung and no one could help feeling that they are under good influences."

Late in November Arthur appeared as one of the speakers in a debate at the School of Arts.[122] The subject was: *"Is betting prejudicial to the morals, or justifiable?"* Along with the Reverends Shaw and Rutledge, Roberts appeared for the opposition and won the day, with the majority of the audience agreeing that betting was not justifiable.

January 1877 carried reports of entertainments by travelling Japanese and European Troupes, who performed in a large tent alongside the Guest's Hotel.[123] Later that month there was an account of a successful gathering at the Public School *"with 300 juveniles present."*[124] Prizes were distributed by Mr Roberts and a variety of *"glees"* performed. The children were addressed by various dignitaries, participated in sports and were provided with an ample 'tea'.[125] The day ended in a display of fireworks before children and parents dispersed.

The columns make mention of politics, sports, the weather, local events, institutions, accidents, illnesses and bereavements. Occasionally they bemoan the weather or criticize district politicians and their lack of efforts on behalf of Scone. Occasionally they fulminate on a topic particularly offensive to the writer. By April 1878 it is tempting to think that

---

[122]   Ibid, 30 November 1876

[123]   The Maitland Mercury & Hunter River General Advertiser, 4 January 1877

[124]   Ibid, 13 January 1877

[125]   Afternoon tea or High Tea

Arthur may have become the regular correspondent because the accounts of school activities became even more detailed.[126]

"The Public School Feast came off yesterday. The children assembled in the grounds at ten am, played until twelve, when they were marched into school for dinner. The school was nicely decorated and very pleasingly laid out for them by their lady friends. Fowls, turkey, geese, mutton, &c, washed down by gingerbeer and aqua pura, made their stomachs, hearts and voices glad. The Rev J. Shaw and several other friends were present. After dinner the children returned to their respective playgrounds and raced &c for various prizes. At three o'clock they were again in the schoolroom and the third and fourth classes, under Mr Roberts, sang several glees and part songs, among which were 'Here in cool grot', 'The bells of St Michael's tower' and 'The labourer's sleep'. Then the little ones, under the able tuition of Miss Adamson, sang several pretty and funny little pieces, which were loudly applauded by the audience. After another hour's play, tea was laid and numbers increased. Over two hundred sat down to tea and nearly one hundred looked on. As regards enjoyment it could hardly be better; each one seemed to vie with the other to create enjoyment, and succeeded ... After tea, the Rev J. Ayling and Rev J. Shaw addressed the children and expressed their happiness that a public school had been placed in their midst, and was doing such credit and benefit to the community. After a few words of congratulation and advice from their head teacher, Mr Roberts, the children returned to the playground to give roaring cheers for the parents and friends who provided the feast. As the shades of night approached so did the band, as now free from their employments they kindly volunteered their aid to make merry and during the whole evening, while Mr Roberts and his scholars were trying by fireworks to enchant the eyes of hundreds of beholders, the band enraptured the company with thrilling harmony. About 9pm, every one had gone home and most will carry a happy remembrance of April 26th 1878."

---

126   Ibid, 30 April 1878

If he was the correspondent during this period, his observations show awareness of wider issues than the local community. One column of June 1878 carries an extensive discussion of deforestation and other environmental issues and implores farmers and landowners to plant trees *"instead of destroying them wholesale."*[127] The same column also mentions the writer's experience in Auckland, New Zealand, lending support to the theory that Arthur Roberts is the author. Other observations, which are expressed in a direct and uncompromising manner, hint at his frustrations and belligerence regarding the conditions under which teachers had to operate.

"What a grand thing it must be to have power and office! And what a glorious position a provisional school teacher must hold, if the following be carried out in every small school. Not a hundred miles from Scone, a teacher obtained leave from the local committee to close school, and attend our Public School feast, on Friday in Easter week, but one of the parents objected, - and after complaining to everyone he met and receiving no sympathy, he deducted threepence (3d) from the school fees for that week, as punishment; also intimating that he would keep his children at home, as he knew the teacher could not keep up the required minimum attendance without them.

What a beautiful specimen of Christianity? Is it not time that teachers who honestly and satisfactorily do their duties, and try their utmost to benefit a small community, should be protected from such mean men. Give the teacher a fixed salary, and do not let him depend upon such low caprices. The country will find that the children of such people will be a curse rather than a blessing."

The column for August 1878 carried the news that the Reverend John Shaw was due to leave Scone.[128] *"I am sorry to say you at Maitland are to get the Revd. J. Shaw; we shall sadly miss him for some time at any rate, no matter who replaces him. May he be happy and if possible, happier, in his new*

---

127   Ibid, 11 June 1878

128   Ibid, 17 August 1878

sphere than I believe he has been here." He was replaced by the Reverend Alfred Thomas.

If there was nothing notable to report, the correspondent employed his wits and feeling for language to create something readable in place of news. One column of this type was penned in August 1878 and is worth quoting to suggest the personality of the writer.[129]

"In the country districts I find it very difficult to get news worth sending. The weather is splendid; Jack Frost comes now and then but not hard enough to nip even rhubarb, and garden plants grow rapidly. I do not remember seeing radishes come to maturity so quick as this season.

I notice that the basecourse of the new post and telegraph office is set, and, as far as I can judge, very substantially. When this building is finished, Scone will have a very different appearance from the train. Mr Dimmock has erected a substantial brick shop opposite it in Kelly Street, which certainly improves this part of the tow; and I think we may soon be classes with towns, without blushing and ruminating that we are only a village."

Other reports carry details of the practical issues the schoolmaster had to deal with occasionally.[130] In October that year a lead coloured snake, over a metre long, was discovered in the Public School grounds, making for the door of the teacher's residence. *"Mr Roberts ran out in time to catch sight of the reptile, and Master Brown, one of the pupils, having a thick stick at hand, soon dispatched his snakeship. Fortunately none of the little ones happened to be near the back door at the time, although generally some of them are on the very spot where the snake was killed."*

In November 1878 the Scone correspondent noted that Mr Bradley, the School Inspector, had paid them a visit.[131]

---

129   Ibid, 24 August 1878

130   Ibid, 19 October 1878

131   Ibid, 16 November 1878

"He examined the pupils of Scone Public School on Monday and Tuesday. Over one hundred children were examined. At a meeting held in the school room on Tuesday evening, it was decided by the local board to again apply to the Council for weather sheds. I fancy if one or two members of the Council of Education saw the playground, sheds would soon be erected. Mr Bradley explained a very neat, serviceable, and cheap pair of sheds and I hope soon to have the pleasure of reporting that they are begun."

The following week there was a detailed report of the Inspector's comments. *"I am glad to see that he was perfectly satisfied, and that all the classes passed a satisfactory examination and obtained a very favourable report."* In response to this success, Roberts was reinstated as a Class 11A in that December. Practical problems continued, however.

"Today is a sad proof of the necessity of weather sheds, for if the children were not permitted to sit in the schoolroom during recess, they would be kept at home; as it is, several pupils are not sent for fear of sunstroke." Tenders were up for plans and specifications for the sheds but they were rejected by the Council as too high. The new year brought a small unexpected relief with the gift of a box of *"beautiful black grapes (sent by Mr Finch of Cliffdale) ... the little ones thanked him very much for his kindness on such a fearfully hot day – thermometer 106° in the shade 5pm."*[132]

In spite of his reinstatement and these happy reports, there were hints of trouble brewing. In February 1879 the column carried a report on the School of Arts that was critical of a performance of the Scone band.[133] *"The entertainment afterwards was enjoyed"* wrote the correspondent, *"but I must say I cannot discern any harmony in the Scone band in the School of Arts. The big drum thrashed as hard as possible, with a triangle tingling; six or eight brass instruments 'blowed' as hard as strong lungs are able, with a nasal clarionette, and shrill piccolo trying to make themselves heard ... I*

---

132   Ibid, 1 February 1879

133   Ibid 15 February 1879

would advise them to see who can play the softest, then we shall be able to enjoy the strains."

If this critique was written by Arthur Roberts, then it is certainly the music master, as well as the journalist speaking. Expressed with force and frankly spoken, it created controversy in the local community and no doubt, animosity towards the writer. There is a general tone of carping criticism in this column and it could be that the departure of Reverend Shaw and other supporters of the School of Arts saw it fall into a fallow period.

The following week carried a special apology to a Mr Bramble, regarding the adverse criticism.[134] But the apology was accompanied by a further admonition to the band. *"They should recollect that if they play before the public, they must expect criticism, and not to be too ready to take umbrage at every little bit of advice, rather than endeavour to profit by it."*

The newspaper, in the interest of fairness, carried a further report by *"a Lady Correspondent"* who reported on a meeting of the School of Arts Committee, chaired by the Reverend John Ayling.

"The ordinary business being disposed of," she wrote, *"the chairman made allusion to some disparaging remarks made by a correspondent of the Maitland Mercury ... with reference to the Scone band; and called upon some of the members to move in the matter. Mr J. Lawlor at once rose to move the resolution: 'That the secretary of the School of Arts be instructed to write publicly to the band, expressing regret at the malicious statements contained in the said article.' The mover stated that the band, originating some months back, had to contend with many difficulties, but with none so great as slanderers who, being deaf to the 'dulcet strains of harmony' take upon themselves the liberty of writing about matters totally beyond their province. The motion was seconded by Mr Salomons. Mr Wilshire and Mr N.F. Asser expressed entire concurrence with Mr Lawlor, and stated their belief that the Scone band would compare favourably with any band north of Newcastle. The motion was then put to the Chairman and carried unanimously."*

---

[134]   Ibid, 22 February 1879

In a parochial community, dissension was divisive and it could be that the departure of the Reverend Shaw saw a decline in Arthur's status in the town and an end to the happy relations described in earlier columns. It may also have seen an escalation in his drinking. Reports in the following months were careful to make only brief and positive comments about entertainments at the School of Arts. April came again and with it the Public School feast. *"We hope to see everyone in town, and out of it, present, and if we are blessed with a fine day, we think we can promise them a treat."*[135]

Some relief must have been provided when Roberts' son, Arthur William Henry Roberts, was admitted as a Pupil Teacher. A letter to William Wilkins of 27 May 1879 notes that Arthur William Henry had passed his examination for appointment as Pupil Teacher and requested that he fill the vacancy for a second Pupil Teacher at Scone Public School.[136]

The Scone correspondent's column of the same month provides further hints that the writer was Arthur Roberts.[137] *"At home in the old country"* he wrote, *"we used to keep up merry makings and picnics on 1st May. I am glad to see it is sometimes kept up here too. Today Miss McLaughlin was married to Mr Gregg, formerly Public School teacher here. We wish them many May days and happiness all through."* The frustrations of a country school teacher are also evident in a column later that month.

"Today tenders are called for weather sheds at Merriwa and Eagleton. When do they expect to get them? Our Public School has been opened three years, very nearly, and there is as much sign of the sheds now as the day it was opened. We do not know whose fault it is, but certainly not the Local Board's, for the hon. sec. has written many times, tenders have been called, sent to the Council, reported too high, called again, and sent again. Since then we expect we are pretty well forgotten again."[138]

---

135   Ibid, 12 April 1879

136   Ibid, 27 May 1879

137   Ibid, 3 May 1879

138   Ibid, 17 May 1879

In a column in June, in reference to the pilfering of fruit and vegetables, the correspondent mentions *"a gentleman friend of mine in Walcha ... We were sipping our wine, when he jumped up in a hurry, grasped his double (shotgun)"* and took a pot shot at someone pilfering his fruit. This reference to wine might make us wonder at the status of Arthur's bid for temperance. There are few explicit clues, except for the fictionalized memories of a young English writer who came as a schoolmaster to nearby Sparkes Creek.

Havelock Ellis was in his mid teens when he came to Australia in 1875. Although it was not published until the 1920s, he wrote *Kanga Creek* in 1884-85, some six to seven years after the events described. In his first year in Australia, he worked as a private tutor for a family in Carcoar before returning to Sydney and matriculating from Sydney University in 1876. After this he taught at Grafton, taking over the role of headmaster when the incumbent died suddenly. Sensitive and well read, he stayed at Grafton for eight months before attending the Fort Street Training School in Sydney. By the end of 1877 he had received his teaching classification. The following year he was appointed to a teaching post at Half-Time Schools at Sparkes Creek and Junction Creek, not far from Scone. By February he had started teaching there.[139]

This posting of the young writer who was later to make his mark as the author of *Studies in the Psychology of Sex*[140] is fortunate for those of us interested in the life of Arthur Roberts. Ellis kept a diary while in Australia and cites his year at Sparkes Creek as the most important in his life. His text opens with an extensive description of his arrival at the nearby town of Scone (Ayr in the book) and of his encounters with the clergyman Mr Chapman (probably the Rev Shaw) and the schoolmaster,

---

[139]   Kanga Creek, Havelock Ellis in Australia, Geoffrey Dutton, Picador, Sydney 1989, pp20-41

[140]   The text appeared in seven volumes between 1897-1928

Mr Williams, a character acknowledged to be based on Arthur Roberts.[141] It is worth quoting his encounter with Williams at length for the light it throws on Roberts, his beliefs and his family situation.[142] We have no way of knowing how much Ellis fictionalized the character but he was a young inexperienced writer at the time and did little to conceal many other local references. As well, some of the description tallies with other reports of Roberts' character.

"The public schoolmaster was a dark, wiry, restless little man.[143] 'Come in, come in,' he said, 'we're just going to have dinner. Queer fish, Chapman,' he added a few minutes later. 'Pretty well played out, his business. He comes here and gives his Bible lessons, but I don't interfere with him; we're very good friends. He's not a bad fellow. Children are quite well able to think for themselves. Only the other day he was talking to them about David, telling them that he was a man after God's own heart. Then I heard my little Jim's voice pipe up: 'If you please, sir, what about Uriah's wife?' 'Hush', said Chapman, 'we must never talk about such things.' But children ain't satisfied when their questions are turned off that soft way; they see through it – they see through it.' He had sat down with his legs crossed and his hands between his knees and moved his foot restlessly. The young Englishman felt attracted by this eager, nervous little man, who suddenly broke off; 'No, I believe in God, but the Bible's a pack of lies.'[144]

'But if you don't believe in the Bible where do you find the evidence for your God?' the Englishman interposed.

---

141   Kanga Creek, Havelock Ellis in Australia, p65

142   Ibid, pp12-18

143   Descendants of Arthur Roberts may wonder at the adjective 'little'. We have no record of Arthur's height but we do know that Ellis was well over six feet.

144   According to family sources such as Arthur 'Bob' Roberts, Arthur William Roberts professed similar feelings to his father. Indeed, in a move unusual for the time, his daughters, Muriel and Marjorie were not married in a church but married from the family home.

'Here!' he returned, emphatically striking his breast with his fist. 'There's no evidence stronger than that. If you or any man tells me to doubt that I just tell him he's a fool.'

'But how do you know you are justified in trusting the evidence of your heart?' the young Englishman was fairly aroused; it was not long since he had found his own heart full of ghosts.

The little man was about to retort more fiercely than before, but at that moment his wife entered, followed by the children. He briefly introduced them. 'Three more children out, nine altogether, and another one coming.' He jerked his head and thumb towards his wife who, with the eldest girl, was busily occupied bringing in the dinner. She was a pale, active woman with no particular expression; if she had ever possessed any clear individuality constant work and much child-bearing had worn it away. She took no notice of her husband's remark. After dinner Williams said: 'I'll take you now to see your predecessor, Gray; he'll be able to tell you everything you want to know about Kanga Creek; I've never been there myself. Gray's not classified, as you are, he has found it pretty hard work to get along, poor fellow, with a wife and two children. I'll leave you with him for a while. To tell you the truth,' he added, 'I'm going to write a letter to the Stockwhip this afternoon – our free-thought organ, you know. And I have some local notes to get ready, too, for the Mercury; we haven't started a paper at Ayr yet. Ever seen the Stockwhip? Of course I don't sign my letters; that wouldn't do. If you ever see anything with 'Anti-humbug' at the end of it you'll know who wrote it. Couldn't find a good Greek word for 'humbug'; they hadn't the thing so they didn't need the word. Perhaps we shan't need it some day either.'

What can we make of this description, albeit a fictionalized one? The character of Williams is feisty, energetic, argumentative and outspoken. He is critical of the organized church and vehemently opposed to what he calls *'humbug.'* He shows a strong liking for the minister, in spite of their differences, and a strong respect for the good sense of his charges, the children in his care. Literary aspirations and some knowledge of Greek are also evident. We are even lucky enough to get a description of Elizabeth Roberts here, aged 36. At the time she was the mother of seven children, with one, Victoria, on the way. Her last two children, Ambrose and Florence, were not born until 1880 and 1883 respectively.[145] Ellis has evidently changed the number of children in the family, either deliberately or accidentally.

The young schoolmaster meets Mr Williams again the following day, where he is given a horse. *"You needn't be afraid of Bushman,'* says Williams. *"He's no buck jumper."* After wishing him hearty good luck, Williams says goodbye, leaving his son, Joseph, to accompany the Englishman to Kanga Creek. After they have gone, Williams and the clergyman exchange a few words. *'I do not think that young man will stay there very long'*, remarks Chapman. *'Well, it won't hurt him'*, *replies the schoolmaster brusquely; 'do him good to rough it a bit; he wants something to shake him up."* [146]

Mr Williams makes his appearance again at the end of the book, when, after a successful and revelatory year in the bush, the Englishman is ready to leave the district.[147]

"Anti-humbug Williams ran out from his schoolhouse door as he saw his young acquaintance alight from Quick's spring-cart.

'You're a brick!' he exclaimed, emphatically slapping the youth's shoulders, 'a regular brick! The inspector told me they ought never to have sent you to such a hole, and I may tell you now that Chapman has been expecting you to throw it up ever since you went out. Well' he went on as he drew his guest into the parlour, chasing out a few of his children in order to gain space and silence, 'and so you're going to leave us for good, and be off to the old country again; I dare say you're right. Australia is

---

145   Ambrose, born 14.10.1880 Scone birth registration number 24162; Florence, Maitland West birth registration number 22435

146   Kanga Creek, An Australian Idyll, Havelock Elis, The Golden Cockerel Press, 1922, p16

147   Ibid, pp65-66

pretty much played out. Things are not what they were when I came out. There'll be a bust-up some day, mark my words. Droughts and theology, deserts and dry bones, that will undo the place. What would old Buckle have said? Curious action of the climate eh? But we brought the virus with us from the old land. Coelum non animum.'

During dinner Williams drew out the youth regarding his future movements: 'So you think of going in for the law? I don't know that you could do better. It's the path to open a career for young talents. I was going in for the law once but my health broke down so they sent me out here – thirty years ago now. Well, perhaps you won't regret the time you've spent in Australia when you've got your chambers in some old court in the Temple.'

The younger man rose, for he had various matters to settle in Ayr before the coach left. When he came back a few hours later out of the hot, dusty road, he found the schoolmaster asleep over the Stockwhip with his head on his arms, and a jug of shandy gaff beside him. The youth refrained from rousing him; but as the coach rumbled heavily off, his last vision of Ayr was a glimpse of the wiry little man running down the street and waving his hat in farewell."

Once again it is a positive, somewhat colourful description of the character of the schoolmaster, who describes himself as thirty years in the colony, when in fact Roberts had only been in Australia for 18 years. Once again we do not know how much is fiction; the references to Williams' writing; his outspoken pronouncements on the state of Australian society; his literary references and Latin quotations. In addition, Williams professes to have once aspired to the law and to having a health problem which caused him to emigrate. What does ring true is the picture of Williams asleep with his head on his arms, a jug of *shandy gaff* (a mixture of beer and ginger beer) beside him. Ellis' portrait is of a deeply frustrated, somewhat embittered man, with a long-suffering wife and an assortment of young children; a man who sought refuge in literary pursuits and in alcohol.

Within eight months of Ellis departure from the district Roberts was officially reprimanded and cautioned for imputing immoral conduct to Dr Creed and Mr Miller, members of the Public School Board. We do not know the details of this *contretemps* but in attacking Dr Creed, Roberts was taking on a powerful adversary. A brief sketch of Creeds' life may throw some light on their differences.

Born in 1842, Creed was of a similar age to Arthur Roberts and like Roberts had immigrated to Australia from England in 1861. After being registered with the New South Wales Medical Board in 1868, he settled in Scone.[148] Like Roberts he was to leave Scone in 1882 and in 1885 he was nominated to the Legislative Council, where he helped generate inquiries into laws relating to medicine and surgery. A man ahead of his time, he opposed the White Australia policy and published papers in support of Aborigines and the Japanese.

At the time of Robert's reprimand, Creed was a practicing doctor and had been a local magistrate and member for the Upper Hunter District in the Legislative Assembly. He was to become one of the leading Australian authorities on treating inebriety and recognized the physical cravings suffered by alcoholics, using the word 'addict' *"in the current sense sixty-seven years before the first usage reported in the Oxford English Dictionary."*[149] His theories, and the opposition with which they met, tell us something about the social standing of people with alcohol problems in this period. The common view was that dipsomaniacs were believed to be *"inherently weak minded"* but Creed believed that alcoholics *"manifested a failure of psychic purpose"*. [150]

---

148   Australian Dictionary of Biography, http://www.adb.online.anu.edu.au/blogs/AO304559b.htm

149   Curing Alcoholism in Australia, 1880s-1920s, F.B. Smith, Australian National University, p152-153

150   Ibid, pp155-56

It is not hard to reconcile some of the writings in *The Maitland Mercury* of 1879 with the portrait of Roberts in *Kanga Creek*. If he is the correspondent for these months then he was becoming increasingly embittered by the active opposition to public education mounted by the Roman Catholic Church in these years. The column of August 1879 states:[151]

"I was glad to read of your leader on the Manifesto of the R.C. Bishops. It seems our poor benighted, pagan, &c, &c public school teachers are not believed to be quite so bad as painted by these clerical slanderers. It is a great pity that parents of children of all denominations do not visit Public Schools more than they do. They would then see that their religion is respected, and proselytism is impossible under the system. That, as one of our clergymen lately remarked in one of his sermons, 'it is not a Godless system.' Every priest, if so disposed, could visit and give one hour's special religious instruction. Why do they not? These R.C Bishops have never seen the inside of Public Schools. Then, how have they arrived at the conclusion that paganism is taught there? From hearsay yarns of interested persons; or have they themselves fabricated the lie? I look upon the manifesto as a direct insult to the whole body of Public School teachers, Protestant and Roman Catholic. It is a mean, cowardly slander, brought out under the cloak of religion. But I am glad to observe that many Roman Catholics see through it. They have had enough of the 'old traditions'. They begin to feel that it is better to live together in love and peace with all sects, rather than perpetuate animosities. These priests evidently do not want the children educated. They are afraid the laity will learn common sense, and argue for themselves. The manifesto has sown the seed that the bishops never intended. They will soon feel the reward."

There was more satisfaction evinced when the Inspector Mr Bradley again visited the school that November and again reported *"very satisfactory marks, many being 'good' and singing 'very good.' The Inspector's remarks upon the organization and discipline are; 'the want of a weathershed and*

---

151   The Maitland Mercury & Hunter River General Advertiser, 9 August 1879

lavatory much felt; otherwise the material condition and organization of the school are good. Discipline, order and general tone of the school, good".

The new year, 1880 brought the excitement of the Garden Palace Exhibition in Sydney. The correspondent reported on his attendance at the exhibition. The weather in Sydney had been cooler, he stated but not so in Scone where he longer for *"the whiff of a sea breeze!"*[152]

"We happened to be in the Public school, which is full of children and visitors, and if perspiration, the use of fans, handkerchiefs etc, be any criterion, we should certainly say it was rather warmer than comfortable. The style of the building for a Public school, in such a hot climate, is ridiculous. There ought to be a wide verandah on at least three sides."

The occasion was a prize-giving ceremony at the school, with prizes of writing desks, reticules, mathematical instruments and watercolour paint boxes. There were also 104 books presented, many *"of a high order"* and, it was noted, selected by Mr Roberts on *"his recent visit to Sydney."*

In his address to the company, Mr Wilshire, Secretary of the Public School Board stated that the school was *"a credit to Scone and also to the country. He saw a marked improvement and was glad to know from the teacher that they had earned, and deserved, the prizes awarded to them."* The Secretary went on to address the divisive issue of sectarianism, coming down strongly in favour of public education.

"He had read statements, from some persons who ought to be above such falsehoods, that our Public schools were rearing children to blaspheme, lie and do everything that was bad. He took this opportunity of denying such slanders; and he was glad to see that the people of Scone, by their presence there, and by the splendid gifts they bestowed on the pupils, denied them also. He knew that the Public schools were the best in the colony, and he hoped that they would go

---

[152]   Ibid, 20 January 1880

on improving as they had done last year and show this not only to New South Wales but to the whole world."[153]

Little wonder sectarian opposition was becoming acrimonious. Public education was enshrined in law in 1880, when the Public Instruction Act was passed, abolishing the Council of Education and the local Public School Boards. In their place a Department of Public Instruction was set up, under the Minister for Public Instruction, with William Wilkins as the first Under Secretary. The Department provided the administrative framework for free, secular and compulsory education in New South Wales, with *"full responsibility for primary education and for the first time ... some responsibility for secondary.*"[154] Public schools, Superior Public Schools, Evening Public Schools, Provisional Schools and separate high schools for boys and girls were provided for. At the same time, the government withdrew funds from denominational schools.

These changes saw a marked increase in enrolments at public schools, with much overcrowding as older style school buildings struggled to accommodate the new students. The inspection system became even more comprehensive, with seven district Inspectors and 15 assistant inspectors. Even with this increased staff, they struggled to deal with the many requests to establish new schools and, as before, they conducted regular and systematic school visits, supervising teachers and trainee teachers, inspecting the physical conditions of schools, the subjects under instruction and the discipline of students. To assist them, local boards became District School Boards, with responsibility for more schools over a wider area.

As these reforms were implemented, the importance of establishing the upper grades became more pressing. The progression from one class to the

---

[153]   Ibid, 20 January 1880; fees were nominal, at threepence/child/week and no more than one shilling per family. Pupils at Superior Public Schools paid one guinea/quarter.

[154]   Education in Country and City New South Wales (Wilkinson) p3; there was a charge of 3d/pupil/week for primary education.

next was based on pupils' mastery of a set of graded reading books and attainment of the higher skills of mathematics. In practice, this meant only the larger schools had fourth and fifth classes. In fact, from 1881 Class 5 *"was generally restricted to the senior pupils of the Superior Public Schools (these) pupils, who had completed the elementary course but did not wish to attend a high school, gradually became known as super primary pupils."*[155]

In Scone, the school year progressed with the usual celebrations in April, where the public school children delighted the guests with renditions of *"Breathe soft ye Winds ... Forgive Blest Shade ... March of the Men of Harlech ... The Canadian Boat Song ... Drink to me only with thine Eyes ... The Harp that once through Tara's Halls ... The British Grenadiers ... Ye Mariners of England ... The Roast Beef of Old England ... To all you Ladies now on Land ... and God Save the Queen."* The children sang *"with their usual sweetness and precision and were highly praised by the audience."*[156]

"As soon as the shades of night began to fall, Mr Roberts distributed crackers, wheels, squibs, starlights, bluelights &c. to the bigger boys, and at once the rain was forgotten; while the noise showed that hundreds of boys, girls, men and women were enjoying the fun. Several large sky rockets and Roman candles, Catherine wheels, and a Bengal light were let off by Mr Roberts; and the whole, which was obtained from Myers and Solomon, Sydney, were considered very good. The wet evening prevented finishing off as nicely as was desired but a very pleasant day was spent and by nine o'clock all was silent, except the patter of the welcome rain."

A column that May, with references to Kent, would lead us to surmise that Arthur Roberts was still in place as correspondent. It was made in reference to a cricket match at Castle Rock and its similarities with *"the ancient castles to be met with in the quiet villages of England and Wales; it is about nine miles from Scone and to all appearances a very fertile spot. Speaking of England makes one regret that so large an area of land is lying nearly*

---

155   State Records, Western Sydney Records Centre, Kingswood NSW

156   The Maitland Mercury & Hunter River General Advertiser, 29 April 1880

idle here, which if cut up into farms like those in Kent and other counties of England, would produce abundance for the thousands, where at present the crows are the only occupants."[157] The match was followed by a substantial lunch *"washed down by the inevitable tea, as well as some really good colonial wine."*

These sociable occasions were matched by others on the Queen's Birthday and by reports of concerts, circuses and the like. Less pleasant was a report in the June column, of legal complications concerning the mill owned by a Mr Little.[158] *"I assure you it is a regular piece of humbug if what I hear is true. As several say, it looks as if the official assignee and lawyer were working into one another's hands. Everyone here, as well as Mr Little I am sure, will be glad to hear that it is all settled."* The choice of the word *"humbug"* may have been characteristic of Arthur, as was possibly the outspokenness on local issues.

Arthur's Scone posting had over a year to run but we have little knowledge of this time. The birth of another child had added to the family's financial pressure but this must have been partly relieved by the wages brought in by Arthur William as Pupil Teacher. The eldest son, David Roberts, was by now a man of 21 and trained as an accountant.[159] Maggie Roberts assisted her mother with home duties and the younger six children, ranged from Albert, aged 15 to the infant Ambrose. This large and demanding family may have been part of the reason for their removal from Scone in April 1882. The new posting to St Ethel's in West Maitland brought them much closer to Elizabeth's extended family.

The Maitland Mercury carried a report from Scone in October 1882 which seems to have a direct bearing on Arthur Roberts and his previous role as correspondent. Once again we can only conjecture about exact dates but the report unequivocally states that the local schoolmaster was

---

[157] Ibid, 13 May 1880

[158] Ibid, 19 June 1880

[159] David Roberts married in 1884

no longer the correspondent for the Mercury. It was in the form of a lecture delivered by the Reverend A.C. Thomas to the Scone School of Arts.[160] The subject was *"How Scone might go ahead"* and, after a lengthy discussion of *"the town and district in which we live, its drawbacks and attractions, its failures and successes, its immense capabilities and possibilities,"* Thomas turned his attention to the lack of a local newspaper. He did not regard this as a disadvantage, he said, since they were served by the *"faithful and impartial ... journal ... the Maitland Mercury"* but his next comments seem to reflect negatively on Arthur's time as correspondent and further suggest that the role may have compromised his position as schoolmaster of the public school.

"There is one thing that I distinctly congratulate the people of Scone about, and that is the advance made in the position of their newspaper correspondents. I do not mean so much in ability to write a good paragraph, as in the greater impartiality with which they will be able to treat all Public Departments alike – that of 'Public Instruction', as well as 'Lands', or 'Works' or 'Mines' or 'Justice' or 'Post Office.'

In very young communities it may probably frequently happen, that a Public School teacher should, by force of circumstances, become the recognized correspondent of a newspaper; and he gets his own copy free for his weekly or fortnightly paragraph, and nobody grudges it him, and all goes well for a time. But suppose that there arises abuses in that school - suppose that inquiries have to be made into its management- then it becomes manifestly apparent that it would not be to the advantage of the public good that the teacher should be the newspaper correspondent, because he must either omit all mention of the proceedings or else give them undue colouring ..."

He continued in this vein, going on to give a short history of the school *"one of the most flourishing Institutions we have, with its roll of 156 scholars and a usual average attendance of 120."* The lecture contains veiled allu-

---

160   The Maitland Mercury & Hunter River General Advertiser, 3 October 1882

sions to problems at the school which we can only speculate about. The following, for example:

"One way in which the (Public School) Boards could be very useful is as Courts of Appeal from an Inspector's decision. The present mode (and why I connect this with a lecture on Scone is, that we have already suffered from the present system in Scone in two instances, and in the country in one) – the present mode is if an appeal is made from an Inspector's decision as to an enquiry into a schoolmaster's conduct, or as to the desirability of any particular spot as a site for a school," then another Inspector is sent, who reinforces the decision of the first.

Thomas asserted that *"if the Board were to hear the appeal … the decisions would ultimately be far more satisfactory."* Bearing in mind that Dr Creed and Mr Miller (both members of the Public School Board) appear to have had an open disagreement with Arthur Roberts in 1879, then we can surmise that the same Board may have disagreed with the Inspector's decisions regarding the schoolmaster.

The subject of temperance was also raised in the lecture and Thomas declared himself a devotee of *"the cause of true temperance"* but reminded his listeners of the teaching of the Bible.

"I cannot preach, as I consider it would be consistent to me to preach, were I to become a Good Templar, that total abstinence is enjoined on, or even expedient for, all. I cannot preach this because I do not find it in the Bible, and therefore I cannot be a Good Templar.

All that I can say further at the present is that sense is being imported into this question of temperance, and that those violent and rabid lectures on the subject which used to be so much in vogue and which did so much to retard the good cause, are toning down. It has been the fashion hitherto for those who were not total abstainers to excuse themselves in this matter – to attempt to justify themselves, as it were, that they needed the stimulant, medically &c instead of standing up and boldly declaring, as I do now, that a moderate use of alcohol, at such times and in such quantities may be deemed desirable, is the course of action that I believe the Almighty intended us all to pursue.

I am willing to grant that undue indulgence, or even excess, on the part of the immediate progenitors of others, makes the tendency to take too much strong drink heredity in some families; makes it expedient, from a human point of view, for a vast number of persons to totally abstain from all alcoholic beverages. But I maintain, when such persons do have to totally abstain, as I believe is the only safe course for them to pursue, they have either by their own vice or by that of their fathers or grandfathers, had to forfeit a privilege which the Almighty classed with the use of corn and oil and which was intended to be a blessing to the whole human race."

I have quoted these comments at length since they give us some sense of prevailing attitudes on the question of sobriety. Events and the habits of a lifetime were to prove disastrous, both for Arthur and his older brother, David over the next decade and it was during these years that the great debates about temperance were taking place.

Maitland 1882

After more than 20 years in the service of public education, Arthur Roberts had to begin again, taking charge of the newly opened school, St Ethel's at West Maitland. The initial enrolment was only 31 but within a month there were 171 pupils enrolled and by the end of the year, more than 200.

Once again, conditions were not ideal, with inadequate materials, no weather shed and poorly drained grounds. Once again, letters of complaint went forward to the Department, explaining that in wet weather, children had to remove their boots because of the mud. From the family's point of view there was no vested schoolmaster's residence, meaning they had to rent first one, then another cottage, the latter in Louth Park Road.

These were repeated aggravations but a far worse blow lay ahead. On 1 June 1885, Albert Roberts died of typhoid fever, just short of his seventeenth birthday. Little wonder such difficult and demoralizing circumstances were followed by a further negative inspector's report in November 1886, when Arthur was advised that *"the condition of (St Ethel's) was discreditable to him."*[161] He was further informed that the school must be returned to a proper state of efficiency within the month or *"the question of his removal must be considered."* At the same time he was reprimanded for the unbecoming tone of a letter he had sent to the Department. His general mood of futility can only have been increased by the death of his brother, David, in May 1887. He had died alone in Sydney; cause of death, syncope, brought on by intemperance.[162]

How did Arthur deal with this succession of setbacks? He was by now a man in his late forties, apparently stuck in what must have seemed a dead-end situation. Despite the independence of his two eldest sons, he still had a large family to support, with six younger children (aged 2-15)

---

[161]   State Records, Western Sydney Records Centre, Kingswood NSW

[162]   Sydney Morning Herald, 7 May 1887, p8

to provide for.[163] According to memories related by some of his older children, such as Arthur William Roberts, his drinking became worse in these later years, when it was not uncommon for him to drink until he passed out. Other memories suggest a Jeckyll and Hyde quality, with Arthur needing to be confined in a locked room. [164] Marjorie Roberts' memory of his treatment of her Aunt Maggie tallies with these descriptions.[165]

It was possibly in response to financial pressures that he took on additional work in July 1890, teaching Saturday music classes to Pupil Teachers of East Maitland. This extra workload undoubtedly created further stress and that October, an inspection deemed his work at St Ethel's unsatisfactory and directed him to use increased effort in the teaching of third and fourth classes.[166]

These were the final years of Arthur's teaching life. He had been in the service of various boards, councils and departments of public instruction for over thirty years. He had never progressed from his original classification and indeed had suffered a serious and humiliating demotion for a period. He had battled to keep schools efficient when buildings were inadequate, the climate oppressive and finances in short supply.

To add to these problems, there was a major flood in Maitland in March 1893. Most of the town was inundated and the waters caused widespread damage, leaving the school in a miserable state. Arthur wrote about this disaster at length in a letter to the Department of Public Instruction that month.[167] The floodwaters had reached nine feet high in the schoolroom,

---

[163]   David Roberts had married in 1884 and Arthur William was in the later years of his teacher training.

[164]   Memory recounted by Bob Roberts based on his father's recollections and supported by further memories recounted by Geoff Thompson, based on the same source.

[165]   See page 17

[166]   State Records, Western Sydney Records Centre, Kingswood NSW To come

[167]   ibid, State Records, Western Sydney Records Centre, Kingswood NSW To come

with forms, presses and tables washed to and fro. Windows and furniture had been broken and locked drawers dismantled, emptying their contents.

"Books, records, clock and other things were washed out of the broken open window. The clock has not been seen since … two of the forms have been found in East Maitland … the stench when the water went down was dreadful and still is very bad … Everything in the school has been destroyed. The books and slate frames in the presses and tables swelled and burst … open. It being so high and the current so strong, all was destroyed. I have of course, applied in the proper form, for books, materials &c.

As regards my dwelling house, no previous known floodwaters were ever on the ground. This last was seven feet on the ground, five feet in the house. I lost everything. The furniture, piano, tables, chairs, sofa, sewing machine, safes, chests of drawers, bedding &c, clothes and even my watch, which in the hurry and confusion was left hanging at the head of my bed.

Three families came in the evening to beg admittance and of course ours being the highest house were offered shelter. But when the water came onto the verandah two feet above any other flood known we packed up as high as possible but the floodwaters rose so rapidly that we all had to ascend to the attic room where we remained from Thursday night until Saturday morning, three nights and two days. Thirteen persons in a room less than 12 feet by 12 feet but we five men could get out and walk around the roof of the verandah.

My horse drowned and logs smashed my buggy; tools etc were swept away and destroyed, my garden and orchard ruined. In fact it has quite set me against Maitland for I have had more sickness in my family since I have been here than ever before and this flood seems a finish."

The school was closed for two months for cleaning and repairs. Not wanting to subject the family to this sort of upheaval again, he applied for a school above the path of the flood and was refused. The Chief Inspector, Mr Maynard, was brusque in his comments. *Mr Roberts's day as a teacher is done but he has a large family and does less damage at St Ethel's than he would at any other 5ᵗʰ class school in the colony.*"[168]

Enrolments at the school lessened as families recovered from the flood and in spite of the attempts at cleaning, the walls of the schoolroom remained damp and malodorous. In the initial stages two tons of coal was burnt over a period of a month in an attempt to dry them out. It was a further year before they were sufficiently dry to be repainted.

Whether it was these difficulties or circumstances of which we have no knowledge, but it was during 1893 that Maggie Roberts showed signs of the illness which resulted in her death on 20 December. Cause of death was *phthisis asthenia* (chronic wasting away) and the duration of the illness, one year.[169]

The following June Arthur was again warned that if he did not show improvement at the next inspection, then serious action would have to be taken.[170] His Saturday classes were closed at the end of August soon after this report. The future looked bleak and his services were discontinued with on 21 December 1894. The following January he was retired under the Civil Service Act on a pension of £139 2s/ annum. Within three years he had died, aged 58 years.[171] His obituary, on 22 February 1898, the day after his death, paid tribute to his active, event-filled life, highlighting his successes.[172] It noted the cause of death as uraemic convulsions.

"As a teacher Mr Roberts had few superiors. He was well informed on all subjects and at the periodical examinations the Inspector was ever loud in his praise of the high standard of efficiency attained by pupils under Mr Roberts' care.

---

168   ibid, State Records, Western Sydney Records Centre, Kingswood NSW

169   See page 17

170   19 June 1894

171   21 February 1898

172   The Maitland Mercury, 22 February 1898

During his career as headmaster scores of pupil teachers were instructed by him and many at present engaged in our public schools owe much to the deceased gentleman ... He was very fond of music and was a good performer on different instruments. He was for some years an organist in England and he initiated a band in Inverell and in Walcha and personally instructed the members."

Elizabeth Roberts outlived her husband by 24 years, dying in Newcastle in July 1922. Arthur had died on the cusp of a new century which would see Australia become a federation. He had lived through one series of revolutions and, like many, suffered the reverses and strains of the pioneering role. A man of obvious ability and many talents, he was father to a large and gifted family, three of whom followed him, with honour, into the teaching profession.[173] One of these was Arthur William Roberts, who was appointed headmaster at Inverell Public School, where he served with distinction, perhaps helping to erase any shadow that had fallen on his father's name in the 1870s.

In many respects and despite the many speculations of this text, Arthur's story will remain opaque. We can only piece together the fragments, hoping they will yield a shifting portrait of this feisty, difficult man, who nonetheless made an extraordinary contribution during a dramatic half century of change. His wife, Elizabeth, as with so many women of her era, remains an enigmatic figure. Her early photograph shows a beautiful and hopeful young woman while the mild-eyed matriarch of later images presents a serene expression, no doubt gained at the price of hard-earned experience. We sense her spirit in the character of the children she reared and the families they in turn established. Their lives and achievements flow back to this couple, who struggled and sometimes failed in their attempts to gain a firm foothold in pre-Federation Australia.

---

[173]   Arthur William Roberts, Elizabeth Roberts and Florence Roberts

St Ethel's Public School.

West Maitland.

29 3 March. 1893.

J. C. Maynard. Esq?

Chief Inspector.

Department of Public Instruction.

Sydney. Urgency removal

Sir.

I take the liberty of writing, not because my District Inspector. — T. Dwyer. Esq? has been negligent in anyway. for he has been most kind to me in every manner, during this Flood time; but that you may know some particulars. that may have been omitted in the General Reports —

In the first place the Flood was nine (9) feet in the Schoolroom. Forms, presses. tables. &c. were washed about, to and fro, breaking windows and furniture. table drawers were dashed open, even where locked. Books, Records. Clock and other things, washed out of the broken-open windows. The Clock has not been seen since. two of the forms have been found in East Maitland. My Daily Report and part of a Roll, with another book I obtained from Mr Callcott the High Street Station Master. The stench when the water went down was dreadful, and still is very bad.

Everything in the school has been destroyed. The books and slateframes in the presses and tables swelled. and burst them open. It being so high, and the current so strong, all was destroyed.

I have, of course. applied in the proper form for Books. Materials &c.

As regards my Dwelling House. No previous known flood-waters were ever on the ground. This last was seven feet (7ft) on the ground, five feet in the house. I lost everything. The furniture. Piano. Tables. Chairs. Sofa. Sewing Machines, Sofas, Chests of Drawers. Bedding

&c.&c. Clothes. and even my watch, which, in the hurry and confusion, was left hanging at the head of my bed, were covered. Three families came in the evening to beg for admittance. and. of course, ours being the highest house, were afforded shelter. but when the water came on to the verandah, two feet above any other flood known, we packed up as high as possible piano &c.&c. but the flood rose so rapidly that we all had to ascend to the attic room, where we remained from Thursday night until Sunday morning. 3 nights and 3 days. 13 persons in a room less than 12 ft by 10 ft. but we, 5 men, could get out of the window, and walk round on the roof of the verandah.

My horse was drowned, and logs smashed my buggy. tools &c. swept away and destroyed. my garden and orchard ruined. in fact it has about set me against Maitland. for I have had more sickness in my family since I have been here than ever before, and this flood seems a finish.

I hope you will not be annoyed at my writing you. but. if possible. please give me a school above flood reach, and as near to Sydney as possible. I have had a fair share of country, although until this affliction, I considered this one of the best schools in the colony. The house, garden and orchard being very good. The next flood may push all away.

Hoping you will pardon me for troubling you.
I have the honor to be.
Sir,
Your obedient servant,
A R Robert.
Teacher.

Printed in Australia
AUOC02n1323150317
283886AU00003B/5/P

9 781925 416374